PALEO DIET

PALEO FOR BEGINNERS FOR RAPID WEIGHT LOSS

Lose Up to 30 Pounds in 30 Days

ABOUT THE AUTHOR

The goal of "Lady Pannana" Publishing Company is to provide you with easy-to-cook, authentic, and tasty recipes.

To increase your health, energy, and well-being, Lady Pannana cookbooks bring together the best of international cuisines and teach you how to cook them in the comfort of your own home.

From special diets to international treats, pick up a cookbook today and lose yourself in a whole new world of possibilities.

No mealtime should be boring, so go ahead and treat yourself!

Browse our catalog of titles and don't forget to tell us what you think about our books. We want to create a better experience for our readers. Your voice, your opinion, and your input only serve to ensure that the next time you pick up a Lady Pannana Publishing Title, it will be better than the last!

To find out more about Healthy Cooking and Recipes visit our blog below

Visit Our Blog => ladypannana.com

You can also stay up-to-date with what's going on here by subscribing for free updates, liking Lady Pannana on FaceBook, or following us on Instagram, Twitter etc.

FaceBook: ladypannana.com/facebook

Twitter: ladypannana.com/twitter

Instagram: ladypannana.com/instagram

Pinterest: ladypannana.com/pinterest

Tumbler: ladypannana.com/tumblr

Google+: ladypannana.com/google

YouTube: ladypannana.com/youtube

LinkedIn: ladypannana.com/linkedin

Visit **our author page** on Amazon to see other work done by Lady Pannana.

ladypannana.com/amazonauthor

If you have any questions or suggestions feel free to contact us at

ladypannana@gmail.com

Thank you for taking the time to read this and we look forward to seeing you on the blog sometime soon!

Cheers,

Lady Pannana

Wait! Before You Continue... Would You Like to Get Healthier, Happier and Enjoy Eating at the Same Time?

Would You Like to Increase Your Overall Well-Being?

If you answered YES, you are not alone. We believe almost everyone wants to have a good body and be healthy by simply start eating clean and diet. Unfortunately, most of us have no idea how to do it. Yes, dieting can work, but starving yourself just leads to frustration and failure. Also, dieting will not help your health! It will just harm you. What we recommend you here it isn't dieting, it is a LIFESTYLE!

Right now, you can get full **FREE access to Low-Carb** eBook+Paleo Report to Learn How to Cook Tasty and More Important HEALTHY Recipes,

so you can easily and quickly start pursuing your goals.

Low - carb eating is something that has become increasingly popular in recent years. It has been linked with a range of health benefits including:

- Improved weight loss (even when you're not consciously restricting your calories).
- Improved concentration.
- Increased energy levels.
- Prevention and treatment of various chronic diseases.
- Reduced blood glucose levels (which are particularly beneficial for diabetics).
- Reduced blood pressure.

Free Bonus

Go Here to Get Instant Access

ladypannana.com/freebook

Disclaimer

All information is intended for your general knowledge only and is not a substitute for medical advice or treatment. You should seek medical advice before starting this or any other weight loss or fitness regimen. We make no warranty, express or implied, regarding your individual results.

The author disclaims any personal liability, for loss or risk incurred as a result of any information or advice contained herein, either directly or indirectly.

All links are for informational purposes only and are not warranted for content, accuracy, or other implied or explicit purposes. All links were working at the time of this eBook's release but may now have expired.

The author does not intend to render legal, accounting or other professional advice in the documents contained herein. The reader is encouraged to seek competent legal and accounting advice before engaging in any business activity.

This eBook may not be sold or given away. Unauthorized distribution, resell, or copying of this material is unlawful. The author reserves the right to use the full force of the law in the protection of its intellectual property including the contents, ideas and expressions contained herein.

© Copyright 2018 by Lady Pannana- All rights reserved.

This document is geared towards providing exact and reliable information in regards to the topic and issue covered. The publication is sold with the idea that the publisher is not required to render accounting, officially permitted, or otherwise, qualified services. If advice is necessary, legal or professional, a practiced individual in the profession should be ordered.

- From a Declaration of Principles which was accepted and approved equally by a Committee of the American Bar Association and a Committee of Publishers and Associations.

In no way is it legal to reproduce, duplicate, or transmit any part of this document in either electronic means or in printed format. Recording of this publication is strictly prohibited and any storage of this document is not allowed unless with written permission from the publisher. All rights reserved.

The information provided herein is stated to be truthful and consistent, in that any liability, in terms of inattention or otherwise, by any usage or abuse of any policies, processes, or directions contained within is the solitary and utter responsibility of the recipient reader.

Under no circumstances will any legal responsibility or blame be held against the publisher for any reparation, damages, or monetary loss due to the information herein, either directly or indirectly.

Respective authors own all copyrights not held by the publisher.

The information herein is offered for informational purposes solely, and is universal as so. The presentation of the information is without contract or any type of guarantee assurance.

The trademarks that are used are without any consent, and the publication of the trademark is without permission or backing by the trademark owner. All trademarks and brands within this book are for clarifying purposes only and are the owned by the owners themselves, not affiliated with this document.

Table Of Content

PALEO DIET..

    PALEO FOR BEGINNERS FOR RAPID WEIGHT LOSS 1

Introduction ....

An Introduction To The Paleo Diet ....

    What Is It? 4

    History of Paleo Diet 8

Paleo Friendly Eating ....

    What To Eat 11

    What To Avoid 20

What The Paleo Diet Has To Offer ....

Delicious Paleo Recipes ....

Paleo Breakfast Recipes ....

Paleo Lunch Recipes ....

Paleo Dinner Recipes ....

Paleo Snack Recipes ....

Paleo Desserts ....

30 Day Mean Plan ....

Links To Studies Mentioned In The Book ....

Conclusion ....

Get Our 2 Audio Books for FREE! ....

Check Out Our Other Books ....

ABOUT THE AUTHOR ....

Free Bonus ....

Introduction

I want to thank you and congratulate you for downloading the book, *"Paleo Diet: Paleo for Beginners for Rapid Weight Loss: Lose Up to 30 Pounds in 30 Days"*.

This book has actionable information on how to use the Paleo diet to lose up to 30 pounds in just 30 days.

If you've been on a journey to weight loss for some time, you know all too well that many of the programs that promise quick results have some major flaw; they are too hard to follow and more often than not only bring temporary results. Think about it- do you really expect that a program that you follow for just 2 weeks and then go back to your 'normal' way of life can have effects that can last you a lifetime? I bet not. That's why if you want lasting change, you have to choose a program that's more of a lifestyle shift than a temporary program that you stop following after a short while.

What then would that be?

Well, of the many lifestyle changes that bring about weight loss, the paleo diet brings about the biggest transformation and this is for a reason; it focuses on making us to eat what our bodies have evolved sufficiently to digest and utilize effectively. It also eliminates foods that the body does not digest and utilize efficiently, which ultimately increases the odds of losing weight and keeping it off as well as attaining a wide array of other health benefits.

If that's what you are looking for, this book is for you; it has lots of actionable information about the paleo diet that will help you to attain all manner of life changing benefits.

For instance, in this book, you will:

- Build a good understanding of what the paleo diet is all about

- Understand which foods you can eat while on the paleo diet

- Understand how the paleo diet came into being

- How the paleo diet works

- Learn the benefits that come with following the paleo diet

- A wide array of delicious paleo recipes that you can use to get started

- And much, much more!

Let's begin.

Thanks again for purchasing this book. I hope you enjoy it!

An Introduction To The Paleo Diet

What Is It?

Also referred to as Paleolithic diet or the caveman's diet, is simply a diet that advocates for us eating foods that our Paleolithic ancestors are believed to have been eating and engaging in activities that mimic those that humans in those days did. For instance, humans those days are believed to have eaten nuts, berries and other fruits and game meat. They didn't eat such foods as grains, dairy and various legumes, which form a central part of our diet these days. The period in question is long before humans had discovered that they could domesticate animals for milk, meat and other products and grow their own crops for sustenance i.e. over 10,000 years ago.

But even with this way of life, our Paleolithic ancestors are believed to have been healthier, leaner and full of energy unlike the modern man who is obese, unfit, fatigued and plagued by all manner of health problems.

Why is that so?

Well, our Paleolithic ancestors lived hundreds of thousands of years to millions of years ago.

When you think about it, you will come to the realization that they really were eating pretty much the same kinds of foods; of course, with the only difference being that some of the things they relied on were seasonal and others were only available within certain geographical locations. Nonetheless, they relied mainly on hunting and gathering, which pretty much got them the same group of foods.

But with the many years that they relied on these foods, their bodies evolved to digest and utilize these foods efficiently without leaving behind any toxic waste, as it takes tens of thousands of years to fully adapt/evolve to utilizing new foods. Around 10,000 years ago, our ancestors started eating new foods like dairy, grains and other foods that they didn't use before. Around that time, humans started doing agriculture and as a result, foods didn't just grow naturally; they were grown and taken care of. Fast forward to the industrial revolution when processed foods started taking center stage, coupled with the use of insecticides, pesticides, genetic modifications and other forms of 'human intervention' in a bid to increase output, make the plants/animals resistant to diseases etc. These modifications meant one thing and that is the fact that people were now taking substances that they had never taken before. This worsened the already bad situation that we had started exposing ourselves to by taking dairy, grains and other substances. And owing to the fact that research on food production is still ongoing, we are constantly exposing our bodies to new substances that the body doesn't know how to deal with. While the body might try its best to metabolize some of them, a good number of them leave behind toxic waste, which increases the toxicity levels in our bodies. This is bad for the body as it can continued accumulation of toxic waste ultimately puts you at a risk of suffering from such health complications as diabetes, hypertension, inflammation, chronic fatigue, heart disease etc.

To be more specific, most foods that we eat these days, particularly the grains are unhealthy and often overwhelm your metabolism. For instance, wheat contains inflammatory protein called *gluten* that our digestive systems find hard to digest, even in people who don't have any sensitivity to eating gluten. Processed and junk foods may also lead to lifestyle diseases or other ailments that weren't there during the Paleolithic time.

The good news however is that you can restore your health by avoiding the foods that our bodies haven't evolved to metabolize yet and taking those that it (the body) has sufficiently evolved to metabolize. However, it is good to appreciate the fact that it is practically impossible to exactly eat what the Paleolithic man ate back then bearing in mind that we live in completely different times than the Paleo man- you cannot just go hunting and gathering whenever you want to eat. Nonetheless, you still can model your diet to eat to eat in a way that the human body can effectively metabolize the foods we eat. To be more specific, "Modern Paleo diet" introduces a wide array of healthy foods such as seafood, fruits, eggs, fish, poultry, nuts, seeds, roots, herbs and non-starchy leafy green vegetables. And if you still can't get over the idea of taking foods that are traditionally made using ingredients that are not Paleo friendly, you can easily substitute these foods with healthier Paleo foods.

So where did this idea of following a Paleolithic diet come from? Let's learn that by discussing the history of the Paleo diet.

History of Paleo Diet

Although the Paleo diet is believed to be at least two million years old, the term Paleo was coined about 40 to 50 years ago. It all began in 1913 when a man by the name of Joseph Knowles went to live in the wilderness for a period not exceeding 2 months.

During his short stay in the forest, he did a simple research on how it was like to live like a hunter and gatherer i.e. the way our ancestors lived during the Stone Age. Joseph had to survive only on those foods types available in his territory, most of them being wild fruits and vegetables. At the end of his experiment, he is reported to have informed everyone how the new diet had transformed him into a healthier and stronger man.

Joseph apparently formulated the idea that the sudden urbanization of US and other countries has played a part in deviation from the traditional living lifestyle especially in dieting matters. He predicted that deviation from the natural foods is responsible for the weakened immunity in many of us and common lifestyle problems such as obesity and diabetes.

Later, the term *Paleo diet* was developed in 1975 by a cardiologist and author known as

Walter L Voegtin through his book, which was titled "The Stone Age Diet". It's in this book that human beings are described as "naturally carnivorous" and thus need a high protein diet to keep them healthy and strong as the ancestral man was. Walter was of the view that since our genetic blueprint comes directly from the Paleolithic man, we should only eat Paleolithic foods in order to remain healthy and active.

Walter also demonstrated how human beings somehow evolved into carnivores i.e. the ancient man hunted for game food and so majorly ate meat, with exception of fruits and vegetables that were available in the forest. Asked about why these foods result to better health, the explanation was that on top of these foods being natural and nutritious, they are also easily absorbed in your body thus are more beneficial compared to processed and junk foods. After the publication of the book, more people endorsed the diet particularly during the 1990's and early 2000s. So far, modern Paleo diet has become the backbone of the healthiest and purest diet any American can eat.

While to some extent paleo sounds like a fad diet aimed at misleading people, science has actually confirmed that Paleo diet is indeed important for optimal health. Here's how the diet can work for you and scientific explanation behind its many health benefits but before we do that, let's discuss the foods to eat and foods to avoid because what you eat will determine the benefits you derive.

Paleo Friendly Eating

What To Eat

The Paleo diet is considered a natural way of dieting that can help fuel and energize your body through supply of proteins and healthy fats while keeping lifestyle diseases at bay. The diet is comprised of limited quantity of carbs and no processed foods at all; both of which form the bulk of standard American diet. On a Paleo diet, you eliminate all inflammatory or "toxic foods" and instead adopt a high protein and low fat foods such as game meat alongside fruits, veggies, eggs, seeds and nuts. While eaten raw, unprocessed or unmodified, these foods help improve your general health.

Let's see the list of allowed foods in Paleo:

1. Lean Meats and Eggs

While meat is top of the list on paleo, you should only buy fresh grass fed, free range meats and poultry. Avoid marinated, batter-coated or breaded variety. To be more specific, you are free to eat the following meat sources:

- Turkey
- Ostrich

- Quail
- Wild boar
- Turtle
- Pheasant
- Buffalo
- Rabbit
- Elk
- Goose
- Pork
- Goat
- Chicken
- Bison
- Bacon
- Grass-fed beef, ground beef and beef jerky
- Lamb
- Organically reared eggs

2. Fish and Sea Food

Fish is rich in omega 3 fatty acids along with other nutrients and thus serves as a good Paleo diet choice.

The following are the recommended fish and sea protein foods:

- Salmon
- Shrimp
- Sunfish
- Tuna
- Crawfish
- Bass
- Halibut
- Tilapia
- Shark
- Mackerel
- Lobster
- Oysters
- Crab
- Sardines
- Red snapper

- Swordfish
- Trout
- Crayfish
- Clams
- Scallops

3. Fresh Fruits and Vegetables

As a rule of thumb, make sure to buy organically grown fruits and veggies as these are free from pesticides, hormones and chemical fertilizers. Also, avoid genetically modified produce or processed varieties in packages unless they are certified to be natural or organic. Ensure that farms, which produce these plant-based foods follow the correct farming rules and no chemicals are used.

When it comes to veggies, go for non-starchy options such as:

- Watermelon
- Zucchini
- Peppers
- Brussels sprouts
- Eggplant

- Carrots
- Broccoli
- Cabbage
- Cantaloupe
- Parsley
- Green onions
- Asparagus
- Celery
- Cauliflower
- Spinach
- Artichoke hearts

Note: **About starchy vegetables**

The following starchy vegetables have high carb content. As such, they can easily make you gain weight especially if you take them in excess. As such, a rule of thumb, make sure to eat these in moderation.

- Yucca
- Beets

- Potatoes
- Butternut squash
- Yam
- Acorn squash

Fruits

While fruits are nutritious and satiating, be aware that they contain fructose, a type of sugar that can lead to weight gain. Therefore, it's not advisable to over-indulge in fruits; rather, limit your intake to around 1-2 fruit servings daily. More precisely, to increase your odds of losing weight, it is best to focus on low-glycemic fruits such as:

- Pineapple guava
- Raspberries
- Blackberries
- Strawberries
- Mango
- Oranges
- Apple
- Lime

- Blueberries
- Avocado
- Lemon
- Peaches
- Figs
- Papaya
- Plums
- Cantaloupe
- Grapes
- Tangerine

4. Seeds and Nuts

These are rich in healthy fats and omega-3 fatty acids but it's advisable to limit their intake. Why is that so? For starters, although they are high in fats, they also tend to be high in carbohydrates. High carb content can stall your weight loss goals especially if you take nuts in excess.

Moreover, nuts such as cashews contain higher amount of fats and this may hamper your weight loss goal. For this reason, try to reduce the amount of nuts and seeds to facilitate weight loss and healthy life. You can eat the following:

- Pecans
- Macadamia nuts
- Cashews
- Hazelnuts
- Walnuts
- Pine nuts
- Sunflower seeds
- Flaxseeds
- Almonds
- Pumpkin seeds

5. Healthy Fats and Oils

Paleo diet is high in proteins and low in fats; therefore, limit your consumption to only those healthy or unsaturated fats and oils. Thus, aim to take fats and oils rich in omega 3 fatty acids, from sources like salmon, tuna and trout.

Here you have options such as:

- Olive oil

- Ghee
- Avocados
- Egg yolks
- Coconut oil
- Chicken fat
- Fish oil
- Macadamia oil
- Avocado oil
- Macadamia nuts

In paleo diet, you'll need to do away with foods such as grains, wheat, soft drinks, fruit juice among others, which can be a big challenge. Therefore, if you find it hard to cut out these foods from your diet all at once, try to gradually reduce the amount you consume until well adapted. It is easier to handle diet change in slow transitions over long term; otherwise, you might lose motivation to stick to the diet.

Let's now see the list of foods that you should gradually eliminate from your diet.

What To Avoid

Avoid these foods:

1. Grains

Foods such as grains are considered unhealthy since they take longer to digest and often yield inflammatory byproducts. Furthermore, their absorption is still poor and thus their nutritional benefit is very little compared to lean protein or healthy fats. Grains also have an active ingredient referred to as lectin, which can hamper absorption of other nutrients and can make them counterproductive to your diet.

For that reason, avoid all foods that have grain in them, whether whole-grain, processed or whatever kind of grains you can come across. These grains and processed wheat products include:

- Pancakes
- Crackers
- Bread
- English muffins
- Cream of wheat
- Corn

- Sandwiches
- High-fructose corn syrup
- Cakes
- Cereals
- Cookies
- Hash browns
- Lasagna
- Wheat thins
- Toast

2. Legumes

Beans, peas and lentils aren't paleo friendly due to high starch (carb) content. In place of legumes, consume grass fed animal proteins such as meat, pork and poultry. You should avoid all types of beans and peas, along with peanuts and other legumes-related products.

More precisely, avoid:

- All kinds of peas
- Green beans
- White beans
- Lentils
- Soybeans
- Tofu
- Horse beans
- Lima beans
- Red beans
- String beans
- Kidney beans
- Black beans

- Broad beans

- Garbanzo beans

2. Processed Snacks and Meats:

Be aware that fast foods, processed snacks and salty foods aren't paleo friendly. Furthermore, artificial sweeteners aren't allowed unless in very little amounts of organic honey, stevia or maple syrup. To be more specific, avoid:

- Added-salt foods

- Imitation meat

- Chips

- Pretzels

- Sauces

- Processed meats

- Seasoned snack foods

- Soups

- Salad dressings

- Hot dogs

- French fries

- Ketchup

- Cookies

3. Dairy Products

If you're lactose intolerant, you shouldn't take milk and if you must, ensure you consume it raw. To make your transition easier, look for alternative dairy substitutes such as almond or coconut milk, which are healthy and are actually as tasty as ordinary milk.

Avoid these dairy products:

- Cheese
- Butter
- Pudding
- Whole milk Cream cheese
- Ice milk
- Ice cream
- Frozen yogurt
- Powdered milk
- Low fat milk
- Non-fat dairy creamer
- 2% milk

- Dairy spreads
- Cottage cheese
- Skim milk

Note: However, you are free to take ghee. While it is made from dairy, many paleo experts agree that ghee doesn't contain the same properties as the other dairy products, as it is made in a process that separates the liquid and milk solids from fat.

4. Alcohol and Vegetable Oils

Alcohol, beer and spirits are all gluten products, which tend to be high in sugar and thus should be avoided at all. Likewise, avoid vegetable-based fats, as these could be inflammatory to body cells and thus aren't recommended for you. Avoid:

- Beer
- Tequila
- Rum
- Vodka
- Alcohol and mixers
- Whiskey

- Sunflower oil

- Corn oil

- Safflower oil

With this information, you can easily come up with all manner of delicious recipes and easy to follow meal plans. Before we get there though, let's go back to the benefits that you stand to derive by following the paleo diet.

What The Paleo Diet Has To Offer

1. Weight Loss

According to the paleo diet, you should take more vegetables and lean proteins. And if you want to really want to live like the paleo man, you should add physical activity to the equation.

These foods are known to enhance a state of fullness or satiety where cravings for processed foods are minimized. With your sweet tooth gone/minimized, you can now eat the right combination of proteins from meat, fresh fruits and veggies.

Like veggies, fruits also help you get fiber, which keeps you satisfied. The fats you get from nuts and various meats also do help boost a state of fullness, as shown by a study done by Joaquín Pérez-Guisado, and published on Internet Scientific Publications. With increased satiety, you are able to avoid foods that add calories or hinder effective weight loss among them wheat and its processed products.

Paleo diet is also effective in weight loss, as it controls carb intake, leading to lower insulin levels. Insulin hormone is secreted in response to rising blood sugar concentrations (after you've taken a meal that is rich in carbs) to help the body to take up glucose since the cells don't have their own internal mechanism of absorbing glucose; they rely on insulin receptors, which in turn tell the cells to open up to take up glucose. If you take more carb than what your body needs, the excess is converted into glycogen or fatty acids and glycerol- depending on how much more carb you had taken. This is what usually sets the stage for weight gain. With the paleo diet though; you naturally take foods that tend to be low in carbohydrates (without even trying to do that). This in turn means that you don't have even enough carbohydrates for the body to rely on fully and as such, it is forced to burn fat to meet the calorie deficit. As the body burns stored body fat, you lose weight. As you lower the amount of insulin produced because of reduced carb intake, you actually end up losing a lot of water weight too, as high insulin levels favors water retention.

Apart from weight loss, other show that the Paleo diet can boost glucose tolerance in patients suffering from type II diabetes and ischemic heart disease. The *glucose tolerance* test is used to estimate how fast glucose is cleared from the blood. According to this study, participants on Paleo diet had significant improvement in glucose tolerance and weight loss. Paleo dieters lost 11 pounds and reduced their waist circumference by 2.2 inches as opposed to control group that lost 8.4 pounds. Blood glucose in Paleo dieters also went down by 36 percent compared to control group that only managed 7 percent.

2. Fights Hunger and Cravings

On top of aiding weight loss, Paleo foods are friendly to your hormones. When you eat foods like eggs, fatty fish, avocado and nuts, the fat content gets into the intestines and triggers release of hormones.

Such hormones, among them the cholecystokinin (CCK) and PYY, help to control satiety and appetite. As Paleo diet tends to be low in carb, it helps prevent spikes in blood sugar, suppresses appetite and curbs unnecessary cravings. Studies show that healthy fats like the omega 3 fatty acids can bring about a greater sense of satiety 2 hours after consuming food. And with less hunger/ better appetite control, you tend to eat less and this alone helps you become motivated to stick to the program.

3. No Counting Calories

Many dieters believe that calories intake has a direct impact on weight gain but the Paleo diet has proved otherwise. Not all calories are equal. While calories from veggies and healthy fats can facilitate weight loss, calories from carbohydrates tend to have greater impact on weight gain especially because they put the body in what I'd refer to as a fat accumulation state because it increases the body's production of insulin, which favors energy storage in the form of glycogen and fatty acids and glycerol. Glycogen requires lots of water to store, which contributes to weight gain. The accumulation of fatty acids and glycerol in fat cells causes weight gain. With the paleo diet, you eat foods that are low in carb and are able to effectively bring about weight loss without you having to count calories. The paleo diet is also high in protein and has some healthy fats all of which tend to have minimal effect on weight gain because they are digested slowly.

4. Offers More Energy

The Paleo diet is a "balanced diet" in that it comprises of vegetables, carbohydrates, proteins and healthy fats, with these foods coming from natural sources.

Healthy carbs from veggies and fats from fish or eggs help generate energy in the body to support all metabolic activities. Even in cases where carb intake is lower, amino acids from protein foods can also be metabolized into blood glucose through a process called gluconeogenesis.

Furthermore, where glucose is depleted from the blood, the liver can oxidize stored fats into ketones, which serve to fuel the brain and other metabolic processes. This ensures the metabolism is up and running even with reduced glucose intake.

Whole foods like fruits and veggies and lean proteins offer a more consistent and steady source of energy that both improves and balances your levels of energy.

5. Paleo Builds Muscle

If intending to build lean muscle, this diet is definitely for you. The paleo diet is rich in healthy fats that are beneficial in muscle growth and repair.

Studies show that supplementing with polyunsaturated fatty acids can help increase muscle size and protein concentration especially in adults. Healthy fats such as fish oil and avocado contain omega 3 fatty acids, which trigger synthesis of muscle protein and repair worn-out tissues or muscles. And based on research, an increase in muscle mass can help boost the rate of metabolism. This can help burn fat and ultimately help you to lose weight.

6. Improves Mood and Cognitive Function

Your body cells and brain cells are made from saturated and unsaturated fatty acids and these cells need a good balance of fats to correctly communicate.

With our modern diet though; we don't get to have enough of the vital fatty acids hence the balance of these omega 3 fatty acids and omega 6 fatty acids is damaged.

Luckily, the paleo diet supplies a perfect balance of fats such as omega 3 fatty acids that is vital for normal growth and brain function. Foods such as wild-caught salmon provide the best sources of these fats and proteins that you can ever get. Fish is rich in omega 3 fatty acids, which contains DHA, an organic compound that promotes healthy functioning of the heart and the brain. It also lowers cortisol (a stress hormone) thus boosting your mood.

Furthermore, omega 3 fatty acids reduce chances of developing brain infarcts and boost mental well-being. Brain infarcts are characterized by small areas of dead tissues in your brain that tend to bring about cognitive problems. Apart from healthy fats, fruits and veggies can help boost your mood, fight stress and bring happiness. These plant-based foods have vitamin B-complex that triggers production of dopamine, a hormone that fights stress, depression and anxiety.

7. Reduces Food Allergies

No doubt, you may experience occasional allergies from eating foods such as milk or wheat-based products. For instance, cow milk is rich in lactose while wheat contains gluten. These proteins can be potential allergens to some dieters.

If allergic to milk, you can develop sensitivity especially if not drinking raw milk or yoghurt where the lactose has been broken down. By default, the paleo diet does not include allergens such as dairy, wheat and other grains. Rather, it is made up of fruits and veggies, which can be very helpful in fighting toxins and allergic reactions. Moreover, the Paleo diet is easier to digest especially if you can't tolerate starch or processed meats.

The diet also entails reducing or eliminating toxic food. Such toxicity comes from eating unhealthy and processed foods that include artificial food coloring, preservatives, added sugars, sodium and other artificial substances. With Paleo diet, you only eat natural food that isn't processed or that which does not have added ingredients linked to lifestyle diseases.

8. Improves Gut Health

Your gut has millions of "good bacteria" that help boost and maintain your immunity, and prevent infections and cell inflammation. However, eating processed and junk food such as sugar and vegetable-based fats causes inflammation and offsets gut health.

Actually, continued consumption of processed foods can lead to health problems like Leaky Gut Syndrome. This condition is characterized by breaching of the intestinal walls where proteins, toxins, microbes and other digested food substances leaks into the bloodstream. When this happens, the immune system detects these leaked substances as invaders and thus triggers an inflammatory response in a bid to destroy them. This is an autoimmune, which can cause various other health problems.

Lucky for you, with the paleo diet, you don't eat foods that could cause leaky gut syndrome and related problems. Instead, you eat foods that promote gut health including those rich in probiotics, which help introduce good bacteria to the gut.

9. Fights Stroke and Heart Disease

The Paleo diet also works against modern lifestyle diseases among them stroke and the heart disease. For instance, a study published on the European Journal of Clinical Nutrition by Frassetto LA et al found out that adopting the paleo diet can help reduce bad (LDL) cholesterol that is linked to cardiovascular diseases. In the study, dieters on Paleo diet reduced their cholesterol level by 22 percent in just 10 days. The diet also helped lower triglycerides levels by an impressive 35% and insulin secretion by 39%.

Now that you know what foods to eat as well as the benefits that you stand to derive from following the paleo diet, let's now discuss how to prepare paleo diet recipes to help you get started.

Delicious Paleo Recipes
Paleo Breakfast Recipes

Paleo Meat Bagel

Serves 4

Ingredients

½ teaspoon pepper

1 teaspoon salt

1 teaspoon paprika

2/3 cup tomato sauce

2 large eggs

2 pounds of ground pork

1 tablespoon of bacon fat

1 ½ onions, finely diced

Directions

1. First, preheat the oven to 400 degrees F then use a parchment paper to line a baking dish.

2. Over medium heat, sauté the onion in bacon fat until translucent. Let the onions cool and then add them to the meat.

3. Mix all the ingredients in a bowl (including the sautéed onions). Mix well to blend well with the spices.

4. Now cut the meat into 6 portions and then roll each portion into a ball using your hands. Indent the middle of the ball then flatten slightly to make a bagel.

5. Put the bagel in a dish and repeat the procedure on the other pieces of meat.

6. Bake the bagel until the meat is cooked through, in about 40 minutes.

7. Then let the meat bagels cool and then slice then into a regular bagel. Fill the bagel with toppings such as onions, lettuce and tomatoes slices.

Gooey Paleo Cinnamon Rolls

Serves 9-10 small rolls

Ingredients

For the dough

1 teaspoon pure baking soda

1 tablespoon coconut flour

1 1/2 cups almond flour

1 teaspoon pure vanilla extract

1 tablespoon raw honey

1 egg

2 tablespoon coconut oil, melted

Pinch of organic sea salt

For the filling

1/4 cup organic walnuts, chopped

1/4 cup pitted organic Medjool dates, chopped

Honey, for drizzling

1 tablespoon organic cinnamon

For the glaze

Pinch of cinnamon

2 tablespoon coconut cream

2 tablespoon honey

Directions

1. In a medium bowl, whisk together vanilla, honey, egg and coconut oil. Then add in salt, baking soda, coconut flour and almond flour.

2. Move the dough to a greased or waxed paper and then cover using a sheet of paper. Roll the dough into a rectangle.

3. Then remove the top cover or sheet and drizzle with some honey, along with cinnamon. Top the mixture with dates and chopped walnuts.

4. Roll the dough in the waxed paper into a log. Put in the freezer and let it harden in about 15 minutes.

5. At this point, preheat the oven to 325 degrees F. Meanwhile, slice the dough log into smaller pieces.

6. Put the individual pieces onto a baking sheet and bake for about 10 to 12 minutes or until golden.

7. As the rolls bake, make the glaze. Just stir together cinnamon, coconut cream and honey.

8. As soon as the rolls are golden, remove from oven and drizzle with glaze. Serve the rolls warm and enjoy.

Paleo Blueberry Muffin

Serves: 6

Ingredients

¼ cup fresh blueberries

1 egg, room temperature

2 tablespoons coconut oil, melted

½ cup coconut milk, full fat

2 tablespoons raw honey

⅛ teaspoon baking soda

1 cup blanched almond flour

Pinch of salt

Optional

1/4 cup chopped nuts

1/3 cup of dark chocolate chips

1 teaspoon vanilla extract

Directions

1. Preheat the oven to about 350 degrees F and then obtain a non-stick muffin pan or line muffin tin with baking cups.

2. Combine together salt, baking soda and almond flour then whisk together egg, coconut oil, coconut milk and honey in a separate bowl.

3. Mix the dry and wet ingredients together using a rubber spatula taking care not to over mix.

4. Now slowly fold the blueberries to form batter. Spoon the batter into the muffin pan or muffin tin to the top.

5. Bake the contents of the muffin tin for about 20 to 25 minutes. Insert a toothpick into the muffin to test it comes out clean.

6. Put the pan over a wire rack to cool down and wait for the muffins to cool down.

Banana Bread French Toast

Serves: 2-4

Ingredients

For the bread

Pinch of salt

1/2 teaspoon cinnamon

1 teaspoon of baking powder

1 teaspoon of vanilla extract

1 tablespoon of raw honey

2 eggs, whisked

2 tablespoons walnut oil

1 teaspoon of baking soda

1 cup almond meal/flour

1 ½ cups roasted unsalted cashews

3 medium bananas

For the French toast

1-2 tablespoons coconut oil

1/4 teaspoon cinnamon

1 teaspoon vanilla extract

1/3 cup canned coconut milk

2 eggs

Directions

1. Preheat the oven to 375 degrees F then add in the cashews to the food processor and puree to obtain a fine cashew meal.

2. Then add in walnut oil into the food processor to obtain cashew butter.

3. Once done, peel the bananas to break them up and add to the food processor along with the cashew butter. Combine in the food processor for a minute to obtain a soupy paste.

4. At this point, whisk the eggs and then add into the banana-cashew mixture. Next, combine salt, cinnamon, vanilla extract, honey, baking powder and baking soda and almond meal.

5. Blend the mixture together to obtain fine batter and set aside. Now grease a loaf pan using coconut oil and pour the batter in the pan.

6. Put the batter in the oven and bake until the bread is cooked through, let's say in 25 to 30

minutes. By this time, the top the loaf should be crisp a bit.

7. Let the bread cool for around 10 minutes and now whisk together the toast ingredients in a shallow bowl apart from coconut oil.

8. Now heat a griddle or skillet and add in coconut oil. Then cut the French toast into ½ to 1 inch slices. Dip the slices into the egg mixture on both sides.

9. Transfer the slices to the skillet or griddle and let cook for about 2 to 3 minutes on each side.

10. You can top the bread with some cinnamon, honey or maple syrup and banana slices.

Rhubarb, Apple and Ginger Muffin

Serves 8

Ingredients

1 teaspoon vanilla extract

1 large free-range egg

1/4 cup olive oil

95 ml rice or almond milk

1 small apple, peeled, cored and finely diced

1 cup rhubarb, finely sliced

A good pinch fine sea salt

1/2 teaspoon ground ginger

1/2 teaspoon of cinnamon, ground

2 teaspoons baking powder, gluten-free

2 tablespoons organic corn flour or true arrowroot

1/4 cup of fine brown rice flour

1/2 cup almond flour

1 tablespoon ground linseed meal

2   tablespoons crystallized ginger,   finely chopped

1/4 cup coconut sugar

1/2 cup ground almonds or almond meal

Directions

1. Start by preheating the oven to 350 degrees F. Then move on to lightly grease or line 8 1/3-cup capacity muffin pan or tins with paper liners.

2. In a medium-sized bowl, whisk together linseed meal, ginger, sugar and almond meal.

3. Sieve the mixture over flours, spices and baking powder. Whisk the contents to incorporate.

4. Now stir in the apple and rhubarb to coat the flour mixture. In a separate bowl, whisk vanilla, egg, oil and milk then pour into the dry mixture. Stir to mix fully.

5. Divide the batter between paper cases or tins then scatter rhubarb slices. Bake in the preheated oven for 20 to 25 minutes or until its golden around the edges. A toothpick should come out clean when you insert it at the center.

6. Remove from the oven and cool for 5 minutes. Then move to a wire rack until cool enough to handle.

7. Serve it warm or cool. You can store frozen in zip-lock bags or an airtight container until ready to serve.

Apricot Power Bars

Serves 8

Ingredients

½ cup chocolate chips, unsweetened

1 tablespoon vanilla extract

¼ teaspoon Celtic sea salt

2 large eggs

2 cups pecans

1 cup dried apricots

Directions

1. Put the pecans and the apricots in a food processor and process to obtain a course gravel consistency.

2. Then pulse the eggs, vanilla and salt until you obtain a ball-looking substance. Then remove the mixture from the processor and add in chocolate chips.

3. Put the mixture in an 8x8 inch baking dish and bake at 350 degrees for 25 minutes. Allow to cool and then serve.

Coffee Coconut Frappuccino

Serves: 2

Ingredients

2 medium bananas, sliced and frozen

½ cup cold coffee

1 can light coconut milk

Toppings

Chocolate syrup

Toasted coconut

Coconut whip

Directions

1. Keep the coconut milk chilled for about 2 to 3 hours or overnight before use.

2. Then put the coffee in an ice cube tray and keep chilled in the refrigerator.

3. Now add bananas to the food processor or blender and puree until crumbly. Add in coconut milk and continue to mix until you get a smooth and creamy mixture. Remember to scrape down the sides of the blender.

4. Add in the chilled coffee cubes and mix until fully blended and smooth. Scrape the sides of the blender.

5. At this point, divide the Frappuccino among two cups and top with the suggested toppings.

Buckwheat and Quinoa Granola

Serves 6

Ingredients

A piece of ginger

4 tablespoons of raw cacao powder

6 tablespoons of coconut oil

1 cup of apple puree/sauce

1 and ½ cups of pitted dates

1 cup of pumpkin seeds

1 cup of sunflower seeds

3 cups of buckwheat

Directions

1. Preheat your oven to 180 degrees Celsius. Then proceed to line silicon baking mat or parchment paper on a baking sheet.

2. Next, stir together buckwheat, and quinoa in a larger bowl. In a small bowl or saucepan, stir together apple puree, coconut oil and dates. Now simmer for around 5 minutes to soften the dates.

3. Meanwhile, peel the ginger and grate onto a bowl. Mix it in the pan with the dates.

4. Put the cooked dates, apple puree, grated ginger and melted coconut oil in a blender along with cacao powder.

5. Puree to smoothness then pour the mixture over the buckwheat mixture. Stir well to evenly coat the mixture.

6. Once fully blended, spread in a prepared pan to make an even layer. Bake the mixture in the preheated oven for around 40 or 45 minutes or until the contents begin to turn brown.

7. Remove the trays from the oven after 15 minutes and stir the mixture to ensure the top doesn't burn. Repeat the process every 5-10 minutes.

8. Once its well-cooked and crispy, transfer the granola to a cooling rack to completely cool down, and then store in an airtight container.

Charred Cauliflower with Peppers and Almonds

Serves 4-6

Ingredients:

2 teaspoons sherry, low carb gluten-free wine

1 tablespoon dark chocolate, finely grated

1 cup & 1 tablespoon parsley, roughly chopped

½ cup whole almonds, toasted and chopped

12 shishito peppers

1 cup canola oil, for frying

8 cloves garlic, roughly chopped

Kosher salt and black pepper, freshly ground

2 tablespoons & 1 cup olive oil

1 head cauliflower, trimmed 1½" wedges

Directions

1. Heat an oven broiler and then arrange the cauliflower on a baking sheet

2. Use 2 tablespoons of olive oil to brush the cauliflower and then add salt and pepper.

3. Broil until the cauliflower gets tender and charred, for about 15 minutes. Remember to flip it once.

4. In a 12" skillet, heat some olive oil over medium heat, and add garlic. Then cook the mixture until its golden, and transfer to a bowl after 4-6 minutes to cool.

5. Over medium heat, heat canola oil in a skillet and fry the peppers for 4-6 minutes. After being blistered and slightly crisp, transfer to a paper towel to drain, and then add some salt to season.

6. Then stir in chocolate, a cup of parsley, almonds, salt, sherry and pepper into the garlic oil; spread onto a serving platter.

7. Use the parsley and fried peppers to top the cauliflower.

Loaf of Bread

Makes: 1 loaf

Ingredients

1 1/2 cups water

3 tablespoons melted coconut oil or ghee

1 tablespoon maple syrup

1 teaspoon fine grain sea salt

4 tablespoons psyllium seed husks

2 tablespoons chia seeds

1 1/2 cups rolled buckwheat, gluten-free buckwheat

1/2 cup hazelnuts or almonds

1/2 cup flax seeds

1 cup sunflower seed kernels

Directions

1. Mix all the dry ingredients in a parchment lined loaf pan and stir well.

2. Whisk water, oil and maple syrup in a measuring cup. Add in the dry ingredients and

combine well to blend fully to obtain very thick dough.

3. Using the back of a spoon, smooth out the dough then allow to rise all-day or overnight. When done, it should retain its shape when you move the parchment.

4. Meanwhile, preheat your oven to 350 degrees F. Then put the loaf pan in the middle rack in the oven to bake for about 20 minutes.

5. Once cooked through, remove the bread from the pan loaf and put it upside down on the rack and bake for 30-40 minutes.

6. As soon as it sounds hollow when tapped, allow it to cool and then slice it. Store it in a tightly sealed container for a maximum of 5 days.

Banana-Nut Paleo Pancakes

Serves 2-4

Ingredients

Dark chocolate chips, optional

4 eggs

2 tablespoons chunky almond butter, heaping

2 bananas

Directions

1. In a large mixing bowl, mash the bananas and then mix together with the almond butter. Blend with the eggs inside the bowl.

2. Combine well and then scoop a quarter of this mixture onto a hot griddle or a flat pan over medium-high heat. Allow time for bubbles to form and then flip, and cook for 1-2 additional minutes.

3. Use a sprinkle of dark chocolate chips to top each of your pancakes to the darkest appearance you prefer, and serve. If needed, you can try a topping of fresh fruit or fry sugar-free bacon as side dish.

Easy Breakfast Casserole

Serves: 5-6

Ingredients

½ teaspoon garlic powder

½ teaspoon sea salt

10 free-range eggs, whisked

2 cups spinach, chopped

½ yellow onion, diced

1½ pounds breakfast sausage

½ teaspoon fine sea salt

1 large sweet potato or yam, diced

2 tablespoons coconut oil or ghee, melted

Directions

1. First pre-heat your oven to 400 degrees F as you grease a 9x12 baking dish.

2. Then toss diced sweet potatoes in the oil and then sprinkle sea salt.

3. Put the sweet potatoes onto the baking sheet and then bake for around 20-25 minutes, to softness.

4. As your sweet potatoes cook, put a big sauté pan over medium heat and then add in breakfast sausage together with yellow onion. Continue to cook until all the pink color from the sausage disappears.

5. Put your mixture containing the meat in the baking dish and then add in spinach, sweet potatoes and eggs, together with sea salt and garlic powder until fully blended.

6. Finally place over the oven and bake for around 25-30 minutes to have the eggs get set in the middle.

Raw Mixed Berry Yoghurt Tarts

Serves: 4-6

Ingredients for Base

1 teaspoon cinnamon

1 teaspoon vanilla extract

3-4 tablespoons of water, optional

1½ cups of fresh or dried dates

1/3 cup almond meal

½ cup macadamias

½ cup pepitas

2/3 cup sunflower seeds

For filling

Raspberries, blackberries and cherries

500g tub of plain coyo coconut yoghurt

Directions

1. Start by mixing the base ingredients in a blender or food processor, making sure that the mixture sticks together when pressed. However, the mixture shouldn't however be too sticky as may not hold together.

2. In tart a pan that has loose a base, press the mix; up the edges of the tart in order to form a tart shell. Then set aside in the freezer in order to allow firming up as you perform on each.

3. Take away the tart from your freezer and then spoon gently into the coyo yoghurt, but allow a small gap before you top off your tart shell.

4. You should top with your preferred berries, among them raspberries, blackberries and cherries. Eat immediately or store under refrigeration to eat when required for at most 2 days.

Paleo Kitchen Pumpkin Waffles

Serves: 5

Ingredients

Maple syrup, for serving

Pinch of fine-grain sea salt

1 teaspoon vanilla extract

1 teaspoon baking powder

1 teaspoon baking soda

2 tablespoons pumpkin pie spice

1/2 cup of coconut flour

1/4 cup of melted coconut oil

1/2 cup of almond butter

5 large eggs

1/2 cup of pumpkin puree

2 large bananas, mashed

Directions

1. Start by preheating the waffle iron.

2. Meanwhile, mix together bananas, coconut oil, almond butter, eggs and pumpkin puree in

a food processor or blender and combine to have the mixture blended with all ingredients.

3. When smooth, add in vanilla, baking powder, baking soda, pumpkin pie spice, coconut flour and salt, and then continue to blend until blended.

4. Use some melted coconut oil to brown the waffle iron lightly, and then follow package directions of the waffle to get the suggested cup quantity.

5. Then ladle the batter into your already hot and greased waffle maker, and spread the batter evenly along the surface. Ensure that you leave about 1-2 inches of border, as the batter should spread after you close the lid.

6. Cook based on the manufacturer's directions, until done. Then set aside onto your plate and ensure it stays warm while you are preparing other waffles.

Crockpot Breakfast Pie

Serves: 4-6

Ingredients

Veggies like: peppers, squash

Salt and pepper

2 teaspoons basil, dried

1 tablespoon garlic powder

1 yellow onion, diced

1 lb. pork sausage, broken up

1 sweet potato or yam, shredded

8 eggs, whisked

Ingredients

1. Grease a slow cooker with coconut oil and then shred the potato.

2. Then add all the ingredients to the Crockpot and mix well with a spoon.

3. Close the lid and cook on low for 6-8 hours to fully cook the sausage. Once done, slice it like a pie.

Turmeric Bulletproof Energy Tea

Serves 2

Ingredients

1 teaspoon coconut syrup

1 teaspoon maca powder

1 teaspoon powdered cinnamon

500ml coconut milk or almond milk

1 tablespoon coconut oil

1 inch of fresh ginger sliced

1 inch of fresh turmeric sliced

Directions

1. Slice ginger and turmeric and then add them in a saucepan. Add in milk, coconut syrup, maca, cinnamon and coconut oil.

2. Let the mixture simmer for about 5 minutes. If desired, you can as well let the mixture infuse for 10 more minutes.

3. Now pour the mixture in a Vitamix or Nutribullet and process for 20 seconds to create a frothy tea liquid.

4. Pour in a glass and enjoy.

Sausage and Asparagus Casserole

Serves: 4-6

Ingredients

Ghee or coconut oil

Salt and pepper, to taste

¼ teaspoon of garlic powder

1 tablespoon fresh dill, minced

¼ cup of coconut milk

8 eggs, whisked

6-8 stalks of asparagus, chopped

1 medium white leek, thinly sliced

1 pound of breakfast sausage

Directions

1. Preheat your oven to 325 degrees F. Meanwhile, grease an 8×8 baking pan.

2. In a sauté pan, heat the breakfast sausage over medium heat and then break it into small pieces.

3. When cooked half-way, add in asparagus and leak, only the white part. Cook the mixture until no longer pink.

4. Once ready, remove from heat and drain off excess fat from the pan.

5. Now whisk together pepper, salt, garlic powder, dill, cream and eggs in a medium bowl.

6. Then transfer this mixture to the greased 8×8 baking pan and then add in the sausage mixture. Combine the contents completely.

7. At this point, bake the mixture in the preheated oven for about 35-40. When done, the eggs should be cooked through in the center and firm.

Avocado Canadian bacon and Egg Salad

Serves 4-6

Ingredients:

Juice from 1/2 lemon

1/2 cup of kale micro-greens

2 cups of baby spinach

2 pastured eggs

1 avocado

1/2 lb of Canadian bacon

Salt and pepper, to taste

Directions:

1. Start by adding in the eggs in boiling water, and let them boil for around 8 minutes.

2. Remove from the stove, allow to cool, peel and slice them into two halves. Then slice the avocado into two.

3. In a pan, sauté the bacon, remove it from heat and place onto a towel in order to soak up excess oil.

4. Now toss the micro-greens and the spinach together with the lemon juice. To add taste,

sprinkle some pepper and salt, and put onto a plate.

5. To serve, half the egg and put one on the avocado and the other on the side. Place the Canadian bacon on the side of your plate.

Nutty Breakfast

Serves 2

Ingredients

1 teaspoon nutmeg, fresh, grated

1 teaspoon cinnamon, to taste

2 tablespoons canned coconut milk, unsweetened full fat

4 tablespoons almond butter, raw, chunky

1 ½ cups apple-sauce, unsweetened

Directions

1. Over medium heat, mix together the above ingredients in a pan and heat the mixture until warm. Stir often until well incorporated.

2. Now add in dried or fresh fruits or the nuts to improve flavor.

Paleo Lunch Recipes

Paleo Copycat Zuppa Toscana

Servings: 8

Ingredients

Scant 1/2 cup Otto's cassava flour

1 1/2 cups plain almond milk, unsweetened

3 cups baby spinach

3 cups red potatoes, diced

1 bay leaf

8 cups chicken broth

Fresh black pepper, ground

Sea salt

1/2teaspoon of crushed red pepper flakes

1 teaspoon dried parsley

1 teaspoon dried basil

1 teaspoon dried oregano

2 lbs Italian pork sausage

2 medium yellow onions diced

4 cloves garlic minced

2 tablespoon avocado or olive oil

Directions

1. Over medium heat, warm up some avocado oil in a large stockpot. Then add garlic and onions to the hot oil and sauté for around 2 minutes, or until slightly translucent and fragrant.

2. Add the sausage and cook for a few minutes or until it is no longer pink. Then add in pepper, salt, red pepper flakes, parsley, basil and oregano.

3. Now add in bay leaf, potatoes and chicken broth and bring to a boil. Lower the heat to medium heat and simmer until the potatoes are fork tender, for 15 minutes.

4. As the soup cooks, whisk cassava flour and almond milk until smooth.

5. After the potatoes are cooked through, add in the kale and spinach soup and stir to blend. Stir to incorporate and cook until thawed.

6. Now add in the milk mixture and stir to incorporate. Cook for around 1 minute or until thick.

7. Serve the zuppa Toscana hot and store any remainder in a fridge for at most 7 days.

Curried Tuna-Chia Salad

Serves 4

Ingredients

1 tablespoon Salba (chia seeds)

1–2 tablespoons balsamic and olive oil dressing

1 dill pickle, chopped

¼ cup onion, chopped

½ cup peeled and cucumber, chopped

½ cup red bell pepper, diced

½ cup green bell pepper, diced

½ tomato, chopped

¼ teaspoon curry powder

1 tablespoon low-fat mayonnaise

1 4 ounces can light tuna, in water

Directions

1. In a bowl, place tuna and use a fork to flake it. Add in curry powder and mayonnaise and fully combine and set aside.

2. Mix together pickle, onions, red and green peppers, cucumbers and the tomatoes and toss

using the olive oil dressing and balsamic vinegar.

3. Serve the salad onto a plate with a scoop of tuna mixture on top and then sprinkle with the salba.

Spicy Cashew Chicken Soup

Serves 5

Ingredients

1 ½ tablespoons of olive oil

1/2 teaspoon of sesame oil

1/2 yellow onion thinly sliced

4 cloves of garlic, minced

1 inch piece of ginger, peeled and grated

¼ teaspoon of red pepper flakes

1 small container of white mushrooms, sliced

2 cooked chicken breasts, shredded

1 cup of water, hot

1/2 cup of cashew butter

1 bunch of kale cut into thin strips

1 zucchini, peeled and julienned

Garnish: chopped cashews and red pepper flakes

Directions

1. Heat sesame and olive oil over medium heat; then add in mushrooms, red pepper flakes, ginger, garlic and onions.

2. Cook the mixture until the onions soften and mushrooms get a color.

3. Then add in cooked shredded chicken mix; and cook until the chicken gets heated through.

4. Add the 4 cups stock and heat to boil, and then add in kales and zucchini. Allow the mixture to boil, then lower the heat.

5. Simmer the mixture for around 15 minutes to cook fully.

6. Combine a cup of hot water with cashew butter in a separate bowl to melt it. Add the butter mixture to the soup and combine completely to allow cashew butter get into the soup.

7. To garnish, use the chopped red flakes and cashews. Serve and enjoy.

Almond and Sesame Asparagus Salad

Serves 2-4

Ingredients:

2 tablespoons of toasted sesame seeds

2 cups of tender asparagus, chopped

2 cups arugula

3 sliced and toasted almonds

For the dressing:

2 tablespoons of lemon juice

1/3 cup of olive oil

1 tablespoon of Dijon mustard

1 teaspoon of honey

1 minced shallot

2 tablespoon or white or red wine vinegar

Salt and pepper to taste

Directions:

1. Boil some water, about one quart or one and a half. While you wait for the water to boil, prepare a bowl of ice cold water to help in the cooling down the asparagus.

2. Then boil the asparagus for approximately 30 seconds on high heat or boil until they are crumby and bright green.

3. As soon as this happens, transfer to the bowl of ice water to help abruptly stop the cooking process; and then drain and let cool.

4. Now in a small skillet, toss the sesame seeds as well as almond slices and then add a few pinches of salt to taste and set aside.

5. At this point, whisk together all the dressing ingredients and then toss the asparagus and arugula in the ingredients.

6. Arrange the dish contents on a platter and top with sesame seeds and toasted almonds.

Turkish Lamb Kebab Koftas

Serves 4-6

Ingredients

Spice Mix

1 ½ tablespoons of dried oregano

1 tablespoon of sweet paprika

1 ½ tablespoons of dried mint

1 tablespoon of hot paprika

1 tablespoon of ground cumin

1 tablespoon of black pepper, cracked

Pomegranate-yoghurt sauce

½ garlic clove

2 tablespoons of chopped fresh mint

½ cup of plain yogurt

½ teaspoon fresh lemon or 1 teaspoon ground sumac.

Kofte

1 medium sized garlic clove, minced

1 tablespoon of red pepper flakes

¼ cup of finely grated red onions

¾ teaspoon of kosher salt

1 and finely chopped medium plum tomato, seeded

8 12 inch flat skewers, soaked in water

1 lb. ground lamb

1 tablespoon vegetable oil

Optional

2 tablespoons of fresh mint leaves

2 tablespoons of pomegranate seeds

Directions

1. Make the spice mix: To do that, combine all the ingredients in a small bowl.

2. Make the yoghurt sauce: To do that, combine all the ingredients in a small bowl

Make the Kofte

3. In a large bowl, put the lamb, onion, tomato, garlic, pomegranate molasses, 1 tablespoon of the spice mix and salt.

4. Then combine with your hands until the meat feels sticky in your hands.

5. Make 8 portions of the lamb (use wet hands to ensure your hands don't stick too much of the lamb) then proceed to press it around the skewers to make 4-1/2 inches long sausage shapes.

6. Then use a plastic wrap to cover loosely before transferring them to a baking sheet. Keep under refrigeration for about 1 to 4 hours.

7. Now you can preheat your oven to 475 degrees F.

8. Then oil the grill and grill the Kofte for about 6 minutes or until no longer pink in the center.

9. Once done, use the pomegranate and mint seeds to garnish. You can drizzle some small amounts of molasses on the yoghurt sauce and serve the Kofte with the sauce if you like.

Fresh Tomatoes with Basil

Servings: 2

Ingredients

¼ teaspoon sea salt

2 tablespoons balsamic vinegar

2tablespoons olive oil

¼ cup basil, fresh

1 cup tomatoes, cherry or grape

Directions

1. Begin by slicing the cherry tomatoes and place in a medium-sized bowl.

2. Then chop your basil finely and add in this tomato bowl.

3. Use olive oil and balsamic vinegar to drizzle

4. Add in some sea salt to taste.

Citrusy Shaved Zucchini & Sardine Salad

Serves: 1

Ingredients

100g tinned sardines, optional for topping

1-2 tablespoon pumpkin seeds

1 medium roasted pepper, sliced

2 tablespoon green onion, chopped

2 tablespoon olive oil, extra-virgin

½ teaspoon sea salt

½ lemon juice

1 medium zucchini, shaved into ribbons

Directions

1. In a medium sized bowl, put the shaved zucchini ribbons and then drizzle using olive oil and lemon juice. Also season using the sea salt and use your hands to toss and blend. You should have the zucchini slightly pickles.

2. Toss through the chopped onions, pumpkin seeds and red peppers, and serve sardine on top.

Basil Spinach Salad

Serves 2

Ingredients

1/2cup basil, fresh, several sprigs

4 handfuls spinach

2 medium tomatoes, diced

½ medium onions, yellow, diced

1 tablespoon coconut oil

Directions

1. Begin by washing and preparing the veggies.

2. Over medium heat, heat a small skillet and then add in coconut oil when fully hot.

3. Now add in diced onions, and sauté the mixture until it turns soft and translucent. At this point, add in the tomatoes and then cook for 2 additional minutes.

4. Finally, add in basil and spinach to the pan and cook for another 1 minute, and then serve it warm.

Kale Caesar Salad with Cherry Tomatoes

Serves: 4

Ingredients

3 tablespoons of nutritional yeast or grated parmesan

Punnet of cherry tomatoes, halved

4 whole eggs, free range

½ lemon juice

Bunch of Tuscan cabbage leaves or kales

1 large brown onion, peeled and thinly sliced

10 rashers of bacon

1 teaspoon coconut oil

For the dressing

½ teaspoon Dijon mustard

3 tablespoons olive oil

4 tablespoons mayonnaise

1 clove garlic, grated

6 anchovies, chopped finely

Directions

1. Start by filling up a saucepan using water and then bring to a boil.

2. In a large frying pan, heat some coconut oil and then add in bacon rashers. Cook the mixture for a few minutes on each of the sides or until it turns crispy. Then transfer onto a chopping board.

3. Onto this frying pan, add in sliced onions and continue to cook for a few more minutes, until turns soft and golden slightly.

4. At this point, add the eggs to the water under boil and then cook for about 6 minutes, or until it turns firmer rather than being soft boiled. Rinse the eggs under cool water before peeling.

5. As the egg, onion and bacon mixture cooks, start preparing the cabbage or kale leaves. Tear the leaves away from their stalks and then slice them very thinly, and then add to the large bowl. Now use lemon juice to drizzle and soften the kales.

6. To make the dressing, mix together the 5 ingredients in a small bowl.

7. Then slice the bacon rashers and then add to the kale and the salad dressing. Use tongs or hands to toss until well blended, to have the entire kales coated with the mixture.

8. Once done, add cooked onion, the grated parmesan or nutritional yeast and cherry tomatoes and continue to toss to blend. You can serve using the halved eggs or 1-2 anchovy as a dressing.

Prosciutto Melon Wrap-Ups

Serves: 4

Ingredients

2 fresh sprig mint, chopped

1 package ham, prosciutto, sliced

½ medium honeydew melon or cantaloupe, seeded

Directions

1. Slice a cantaloupe carefully into 1 inch wedges and then take out the rinds.

2. Use the prosciutto to wrap each of the cantaloupes and then use toothpicks to secure if necessary.

3. You can garnish with fresh mint, and then serve it at room temperature or when cooled.

Slow Cooker Beef Minestrone

Serves: 7

Ingredients

6 ounces of baby spinach

1 can of tomato paste

20 ounces of water

1 can diced tomatoes

32 ounce of beef stock

2 ounce each for carrots, onions and cabbages

2 tablespoons olive oil

2 cubed chuck roast, fat trimmed

To taste: pepper, thyme, oregano, basil, garlic powder, onion powder

Directions

1. In a heavy skillet, heat oil and then seer beef cubes. Remove from slow cooker and add seasonings and vegetables.

2. Then sauté until they are crisp-tender before adding to the slow cooker.

3. Combine water and tomato paste to the slow cooker together with the stock and tomatoes.

4. Now cook under low heat for about 8 hours before adding spinach. Then cook for additional 5 minutes or until they wilt, and serve.

Turkey Carrot Quiche

Serves 4

Ingredients

1 tablespoon of coconut oil or bacon fat

½ teaspoon black pepper

½ teaspoon sea salt

¼ cup water

¼ cup herbs, fresh, chopped like basil and parsley

¼ teaspoon cumin

1 teaspoon mustard, Dijon

1 medium onion, chopped

1 cup carrot, shredded

½ pound turkey, ground

8 large eggs

Directions

1. Preheat the oven to 350 degrees F. Grease a 9-inch dish or pie plate using coconut oil or bacon fat. Set aside.

2. In a pan, brown the cumin, Dijon mustard, carrots, onions and ground turkey.

3. Let the turkey mixture to slightly cool as you whisk the eggs in a bowl.

4. Add in the cooled turkey, water, pepper, salt and the herbs to the eggs and continue to whisk together.

5. Pour this mixture into a baking dish or pie plate and cook for around 45 minutes. Once set, serve.

Creepy Green Soup

Serves 4

Ingredients

2 cups cold water

2 tablespoons of lemon juice

1/4 cup fresh mint leaves

1 large cucumber, peeled and chopped

1 avocado

4 green onions, chopped

1/4 pound of spinach, with the stems removed

1/2 pound asparagus, cut into 2 inch pieces

Directions

1. In a blender, puree the asparagus using ½ cup of water until its smooth.

2. Add the spinach, green onions and cucumber, with ½ cup water. Blend a second time to puree.

4. Add in lemon juice, mint and avocado and continue to blend using the water that remains.

5. Use the ground pepper that remains to season and continue to blend.

6. If desired, add some coconut milk or a heavy cream on top and serve immediately.

Chili-Beef Kebabs

Serves 8

Ingredients

2 tablespoons of parsley

8 medium scallions or spring onions

1/8 teaspoon red or cayenne pepper

1 teaspoon salt

1 tablespoon chili powder

3 teaspoons garlic

2 tablespoons canola vegetable oil

2 lb. beef top sirloin

Directions

1. Mix together red pepper, salt, chili powder, garlic and oil in a bowl.

2. Add in green onions and beef, and toss to coat. Marinate the contents for about 1 hour.

3. Now soak the skewers in water or thread the green onion pieces and beef on the skewers.

4. Prepare a medium-heat grill and grill the kebabs for about 10-15 minutes, while turning occasionally.

5. Once done, sprinkle with parsley and enjoy.

Green Noodle Salad

Serves 2

Ingredients

1 pinch of pepper

1 pinch of sea salt

1 cup chopped fresh basil

2 tablespoons of lemon juice, fresh

¼ cup yeast-free vegetable stock

1 garlic clove

100 g broccoli

100 g zucchini

100 g fresh spinach

100 g millet noodles

Directions

1. First cook the noodles based on the package directions, then drain and rinse them using cold running water. Set aside and allow to cool.

2. Then cut the zucchini into thin slices and chop the broccoli. Steam them very lightly for a

few minutes until the color pops. Ensure they still remain crunchy.

3. Now chop basil, then wash and cut the spinach to eliminate the stems.

4. To prepare a dressing, combine vegetable stock and lemon juice in a mixer, then add in chopped garlic and continue to mix for 15-30 seconds.

5. Now mix the basil, chopped spinach, zucchini, broccoli and noodles in a bowl and pour over the dressing. Ensure that you mix well and season with pepper and salt.

Turkey Bacon and Sweet Potato Hash

Serves 1

Ingredients

Pepper, freshly ground

Sea salt

1 tablespoon water

2 whole eggs

1/2 cup red or green pepper, diced

2-3 turkey sausages or turkey bacon, nitrate-free; sliced

¼ cup sweet onion, diced

½ medium sweet potato, cubed

1 teaspoon coconut oil, divided

Directions

1. Heat coconut oil in a large skillet over medium heat and then add in sweet potatoes and onions, and sauté for around 5 minutes.

2. Add in sausages and continue with the cooking to have the sausages turn brown and the sweet potatoes soften slightly.

3. Add in water and bell peppers, cover and continue to cook until sweet potatoes gets completely soft, in about 15 minutes; while stirring regularly.

4. Once done, remove from heat and enjoy your meal.

Beet the Detox Salad

Servings: 4

Ingredients

4 cups mixed greens

2 tablespoons lemon juice

2 tablespoons flax, pumpkin, hemp or seed oil

2 tablespoons almonds, chopped

1 large apple, diced

1 large carrot, coarsely grated

1 large beet, coarsely grated

Optional

1/4 teaspoon gray sea salt or pink rock salt

2 garlic cloves, minced

2 tablespoons fresh dill or parsley, finely chopped

Directions

1. Toss all the other ingredients apart from the mixed greens in a large bowl.

2. Then add in the optional add-ons if desired. Alternatively, you can prepare the dressing 2 days in advance and keep in the fridge.

3. Divide the salad greens between 4 plates and top with the apple mixture if desired.

Pesto Zucchini Noodles

Serves 4

Ingredients

2-3 tablespoons prepared basil pesto

2 cups broccoli florets

1/2 cup green onions cut into 1-inch pieces

6 slices of uncooked bacon

Pinch of salt

4 medium zucchini, julienned thinly

Directions:

1. Put the zucchini in a colander in the sink or over a bowl and then sprinkle with salt. Toss to combine.

2. Let the toasted zucchini to sit for about 15 minutes then drain the excess water by squeezing the zucchini.

3. Over medium heat, cook the bacon in a skillet until crisp, as you turn it regularly. Then remove the bacon to paper towels to dry.

4. Now crumble the bacon and remove the bacon drippings; but reserve about 2 tablespoons of the drippings.

5. Then return the pan to heat and add in broccoli and green onions. Stir frequently and cook under medium heat until crisp tender, in about 3-5 minutes.

6. Add in 2 tablespoons of pesto and zucchini and toss to combine. Taste and adjust the seasonings as desired and let it warm up for 2-3 minutes.

7. Top with bacon crumbles.

Paleo Dinner Recipes

Tex-Mex Turkey Skillet

Serves: 4

Ingredients

Black pepper, freshly ground

Sea salt

Cooking fat (paleo friendly)

Pickled jalapeños

1 teaspoon of cumin

2 teaspoons of smoked paprika

2 tablespoons chili powder

1/2 cup chicken stock

1 1/2 cups enchilada sauce

1 avocado, diced

4 green onions, sliced

2 garlic cloves, minced

1 onion, diced

1 cup grape tomatoes, halved

1 bell pepper, chopped

2 cups leftover turkey, shredded

Directions

1. In a skillet, melt cooking oil over medium high heat. Then add in garlic and onions and cook for a few seconds, or until soft.

2. Stir in half of the green onions, tomatoes and bell pepper. Then top with cumin, paprika, chili powder, pepper and salt.

3. Stir the mixture and cook for about 3 to 4 minutes. Once done, add in chicken stock, enchilada sauce and turkey.

4. Bring the dish to a boil, and then reduce the heat. Cover and let the contents simmer for around 20 to 25 minutes.

5. Serve with pickled jalapenos, avocados and the rest of the green onions.

Paleo Pineapple Fried Rice

Serves: 4

Ingredients

4 eggs

1 head of cauliflower

1 bunch of green onions, thinly sliced

2 cloves garlic, minced

4 small carrots

1 red bell pepper

2 cups of fresh pineapple, cut into small chunks

¼ cup avocado oil

Sauce:

2 teaspoons of chili paste

¼ cup coconut aminos

To finish:

Sea salt

1 cup roasted cashew pieces

Directions

1. Start by cutting the bell pepper lengthwise to create thick strips of 1/2 inch thickness then proceed to cut the strips crosswise into long pieces (½ inch).

2. Then peel the carrots. Cut off the ends and slice them thin. Use a grater to grate the cauliflower then set it aside.

3. In a bowl, crack the eggs and then lightly whisk them using a fork. In a small bowl, combine chili paste and coconut aminos and set the mixture aside.

4. At this point, preheat a large skillet over medium-high heat until it's hot. Then add in a tablespoon of avocado oil.

5. Now sear the pineapple chunks to caramelize the edges in about 2 or 3 minutes. Remove the seared pineapples from the skillet and set aside.

6. Then add in 3 tablespoons of oil to the pan and cook the garlic, carrots and bell pepper until the veggies are crisp tender.

7. Add in cauliflower and green onions to the pan and cook until the cauliflower is soft, in about 1 to 2 minutes.

8. Then add in the eggs and let cook for around 1 to 2 minutes. As soon as the eggs scrambles, add the sauce and cook until the sauce is absorbed and fully mixed in, or for another 1 to 2 minutes.

9. At this point, remove the cauliflower from heat and add in the caramelized pineapple and the cashews.

10. Adjust the seasonings as you like it then serve and enjoy.

Paleo Pizza Chicken

Serves 4

Ingredients

1 tablespoon pizza seasoning

2 teaspoons salt

1-2 tablespoon extra-virgin olive oil

24-30 slices uncured pepperoni

1/2 cup pizza sauce, sugar free

8 chicken thighs

Directions

1. Preheat the oven to around 425 degrees F and then put chicken thighs in a pan, preferably a 13x9.

2. Remove the skin from each chicken meat and then add 1 to 2 tablespoons of the sauce on the thighs.

3. Top each of the thighs with 4 to 5 slices of the pepperoni, before pulling the skin back on so that you cover the sauce and pepperoni.

4. Now drizzle the oil on the thigh and season with pizza seasoning and some salt.

5. Bake the meat until the skin is browned, or for about 40 to 50 minutes.

Lebanese Lemon Chicken

Serves: 6-8

Ingredients

2 sprigs of fresh thyme

2 sprigs of fresh rosemary

2 large shallots or 1 large onion

3 pounds boneless, skinless chicken thighs

Black pepper, freshly ground

1½ teaspoons flaky sea salt

1/2 teaspoon ground turmeric

2 tablespoons extra virgin olive oil

3 organic lemons

Directions

1. Obtain 2 tablespoons of lemon juice then put the juice in a large bowl along with black pepper, sea salt and turmeric.

2. Add chicken to the bowl and toss to blend with the seasonings. Allow the thighs to marinate for a few minutes.

3. Then proceed to cut off the ends of 2 lemons before slicing them into rounds of ¼ inch thick.

4. Next, half and peel the shallots, then discard the seeds before slicing the deseeded shallots.

5. Over medium-high heat, warm two large cast irons then add olive oil so that it coats the bottom. Divide the thighs between two pans with the skin side of the chicken facing own.

6. Cook the chicken thighs until nicely browned on the bottom, in about 5 minutes. Flip and cook the other side for about 8 to 10 minutes. If need be, reduce the heat to allow the meat to brown.

7. At this point, move the meat to a plate using slotted spatula or a pair of tongs. Then add in herb sprigs, shallots and the lemons to the pan.

7. Allow the ingredients to cook for 3 to 4 minutes or until the lemons are brown. Now pour half cup of water into every pan and stir as you scrap the browned bits from the pan.

8. Lower the heat to medium, and then add in the meat to the pans. Cook until the flavors meld, in about 4 to 5 minutes.

9. You can now serve the lemon chicken with pan juices and shallots over cauliflower rice.

Chorizo & Vegetable Stew

Serves: 3

Ingredients

1 medium zucchini, diced

1 tablespoon of lemon juice

2 cups of chicken stock or bone broth

2 large garlic cloves, diced

1 large tomato, diced

2 medium white potatoes, peeled and diced

1 large celery stick, sliced

1 large pointy red pepper, seeds out and diced

1 large carrot, sliced

2 medium chorizo sausages, skin peeled off and sliced

1 large brown onion, roughly diced

1 tablespoon of coconut oil

Handful of fresh parsley, chopped

Pepper

Sea salt

Directions

1. In a medium saucepan, heat coconut oil over medium high heat. Then add in celery, carrots, chorizo and onions.

2. Sauté until slightly softened and golden, or for about 2 to 3 minutes, while stirring frequently. By now the chorizo should have released some fat, which you will use to cook the veggies.

3. Add the garlic, tomatoes, red peppers and potato and stir through for around 1 minute.

4. Pour in lemon juice and the stock, stir and seal the lid in place. Bring the liquids to a boil then set the heat to medium. Cover and cook for 10 minutes or until the potato has softened and the sauce thickens.

5. Now open the lid and bring the contents to medium high heat for around 2 minutes, while stirring through.

6. Remove from heat and sprinkle chopped parsley on top. Serve with sautéed or steamed greens

Chicken with Fig and Shallot Compote

Serves 4-6

Ingredients

1 pint figs, finely chopped

3 shallots, halved and thinly sliced

1 lemon

Black pepper, freshly ground

2 teaspoons ghee or extra virgin olive oil

1 teaspoon flaky sea salt

8 bone-in, skin-on chicken thighs

Directions

1. Heat the oven to 450 degrees F. Meanwhile, season all sides of the chicken with salt.

2. Heat a large skillet and then add oil or ghee to the hot pan. Coat the bottom of the pan with oil then add in the chicken, with the skin side facing down.

3. Season the chicken with pepper and cook over medium-high heat until the chicken is deep golden brown, or for about 10 minutes.

4. Once done, turn off the heat, flip over the meat and then season the skin side using pepper.

5. Move the skillet to the oven and roast until the chicken is cooked through, or for around 20 to 25 minutes.

6. As the chicken roasts, zest the lemon to make thin strips before you juice it to obtain about 2 tablespoons of juice.

7. Now remove the roasted chicken from the oven and move the meat from the skillet to a plate. Cover using a foil to cool down.

8. Pour off all the fat from the skillet reserving only a tablespoon. Over medium-high heat, add half of the lemon zest and the shallots to the pan.

9. Cook the mixture until the shallots have softened, or for about 5 minutes. Remember to scrap the bottom of the pan using a spatula.

10. Lower the heat to medium then add in the figs to the pan. Cook the mixture for about 2 to 3 minutes or until the figs are heated through; while stirring frequently.

11. At this point, stir in a tablespoon of lemon juice and taste the dish. Adjust the seasonings i.e. lemon juice, salt and pepper.

12. Serve the meat hot with warm compote drizzled on top. You can garnish with lemon wedges or lemon zest if you like.

Paleo Mini Meatloaves

Serves 6

Ingredients

1/4 teaspoon grated nutmeg

1 teaspoon dried thyme

1 teaspoon garlic powder

2 teaspoons onion powder

2 teaspoons pepper

2 teaspoons salt

1/3 cup coconut flour

4 eggs, lightly beaten

2 carrots, grated or finely diced

6 ounces mushrooms, finely diced

1 medium onion, finely diced

1-2 teaspoons oil

10 ounces frozen, chopped spinach

2 pounds ground meat –beef or pork

Directions

1. First, preheat your oven to 375 degrees F.

2. Then thaw the spinach, squeeze out the extra water and set it aside. Over medium heat, warm a pan then add oil.

3. Once hot, fry the mushrooms and onions until some liquid has cooked out of the mushrooms and the onions are translucent. Set the mixture aside to cool.

4. Now put the ground meat in a large bowl and add in coconut flour, beaten eggs, onion and mushroom mixture, spinach and all the spices. Combine well using your hands.

5. At this point, fill 18 regularly sized muffin pans or tins with the batter. You may need to grease the muffin tins beforehand.

6. Cook the meatloaf until the internal temperature reaches 160 degrees, in about 20 to 30 minutes.

7. Let the meatloaf cool and then loosen it from the sides of the pan using a knife. Serve with marinara sauce that hasn't been artificially sweetened.

Grilled Chicken Satay

Serves: 2

Ingredients

For Chicken

Skewers

2 chicken breasts, boneless, skinless; 1 inch chunks

For Sauce

1/2 teaspoons red pepper flakes

2 garlic cloves chopped

1 teaspoons ginger, freshly ground

2 tablespoons coconut aminos

1 lime or 2 tablespoons lime juice

1 cup coconut milk

1/2 cup sunflower seed butter

Directions

1. In a blender or a food processor, put the ingredients for sauce and then combine until smooth to the consistency of a smoothie mixture.

2. Scoop about a 1/3 of the sauce to marinate the chicken chunks or the whole chicken in the fridge for about 3 hours to 48 hours.

3. Once prepared to cook the chicken, continue to preheat your grill for around 10 minutes for high and then turn down heat to medium i.e. 450-500 degrees F.

4. Slam the chicken using the skewers while on the grill and continue to cook for 6 minutes on each of the sides until it's done.

5. You can serve over a bed of cauliflower couscous garnished with pineapple or with freshly sautéed vegetables.

Ground Beef Stroganoff

Serves 4-6

Ingredients

1/2 teaspoon of black pepper

1/2 teaspoon of sea salt

2/3 cup thick coconut cream

1 1/2 cup beef stock

1 tablespoons arrowroot powder

4 cloves of garlic

1 1/2 teaspoons rosemary

1 1/2 teaspoons thyme

2 tablespoons of tomato paste

1 pound of beef, ground

8 ounces of white mushrooms, sliced

1 large onion, diced

2 tablespoons of olive oil or coconut oil, extra-virgin

2 tablespoons of ghee

Directions

1. Melt some ghee in a skillet using about a teaspoon of coconut or olive oil and then add in the onions along with the mushrooms. Sauté for a few seconds until the edges turn brown and are soft then set aside in a bowl.

2. Brown your beef in a tablespoon of olive or coconut oil until it's no longer pink. Then return the mushroom and onion mixture to the pan and add in garlic, rosemary, thyme and tomato paste.

3. Sauté the mixture for 3 more minutes to allow the flavors to form and then lower the heat to medium.

4. Over the meat mixture, sprinkle the arrowroot powder until the arrowroot is fully mixed in. Then add the beef stock and continue to mix in.

5. Allow the mixture to simmer for the sauce to thicken and then lower the heat to simmer for 5 additional additions. Take out from the heat and allow to cool for a few minutes.

6. At this point, stir in the coconut cream; and serve over sweet potato noodle, cauliflower rice, sliced zucchini noodles or with roasted Spaghetti Squash and roasted veggies.

Lamb Sliders with Ginger Cilantro Aioli

Serves 6-8

Ingredients

For Lamb Sliders

1 tablespoon bacon fat

2 garlic cloves, minced

1 teaspoon black pepper

1 teaspoon sea salt

2 pounds ground grass fed lamb

Garnishes for sliders; Dill pickles, romaine lettuce, red onion and Roma tomatoes

For Sweet Potato "Bun"

Oregano

Pepper

Italian seasoning

Garlic powder

Sea salt

3 white sweet potatoes, peeled; 1/4 inch thick slices

For Ginger Cilantro Aioli

1 teaspoon fresh ginger, grated

1 teaspoon diced jalapeño

1 cup homemade mayo

1 lime juice

2 tablespoons cilantro, minced

Directions

1. Use the garlic, pepper and salt to season the lamb meat and combine together using your hands to make your sliders. You can made around 12 sliders that are about ½-inch thick and 4 inches to match to the shape of the sweet potato "burn"

2. In a large skillet, warm bacon grease over medium heat and then cook the sliders for around 3-5 minutes on each side. Be careful as the lamp normally cooks fast; you shouldn't overcook.

3. Prepare to make the sweet potato buns by preheating your oven to 375 degrees F. Use Italian seasoning, oregano, pepper, garlic powder and sea salt to season the sliced white sweet potatoes.

4. Use coconut oil to coat a baking sheet and then put the seasoned slices onto the baking sheet. Then bake in the preheated oven for around 10 minutes, and flip them over. Continue to cook for 10-15 additional minutes or until it's done.

5. Once done with baking, allow the sweet potato buns to rest for a moment.

6. To prepare the ginger cilantro aioli, combine the 5 ingredients in a bowl starting with fresh ginger, diced jalapeño, homemade mayo, cilantro and juice from a lemon.

7. Then assemble the sliders, and spread some of the ginger cilantro aioli onto your sweet potato buns. Now add in a slider and use your favorite Paleo garnish.

Crab and Avocado Salad

Serves 4

Ingredients

3 cups of chopped watercress

1 California avocado

2 stalks medium celery

16 oz. canned crab

1/2 teaspoon paprika

1 teaspoon cumin

2 tablespoons of fresh lime juice

3 tablespoons of real mayonnaise

Directions

1. Combine paprika, cumin, lime juice and mayonnaise in a large bowl.

2. Add in diced celery and crab meat then mix well. Season the mixture with black pepper and salt.

3. Then stir in avocado cubes. Divide watercress among plates and top with salad.

Cod with Olives and Lemon

Serves 4

Ingredients

1 teaspoon lemon peel

24 oz. boneless cod

1 1/4 oz. pitted kalamata olives

1 fl oz lemon juice

4 tablespoons of ghee

Directions

1. Obtain juice from the lemon and dice the olives. Add ghee and combine using a fork.

2. Add in salt, pepper, lemon zest and 2 tablespoons lemon juice. Mix to blend.

3. Over medium-high heat, add oil to a skillet and sauté broccoli for about 5-6 minutes or until softened.

4. At this point, season the cod with salt and pepper. Broil or grill for around 3-4 minutes on each side, or until its white and firm.

5. Move the fish to the plate with broccoli, and top with a quarter of olive ghee mixture.

Pumpkin Ratatouille

Serves 4

Ingredients

1 cup of water

Pinch of pepper

Sea salt or organic salt

4 tablespoons of extra-virgin olive oil, cold pressed

2 teaspoons of herbs de Provence

2 cloves of garlic

2 big onions

1/2 lb tomatoes

1 red bell pepper

1 yellow bell pepper

1 lb fresh pumpkin

Directions

1. Cut the bell pepper, tomatoes and the pumpkin flesh into bit-sized portions. Then dice the garlic and onion.

2. In a pot, heat some olive oil and then sauté the garlic and onion for a few minutes.

3. Now add in the bell pepper and pumpkin and stir-fry the mixture for approximately 8 minutes.

4. When done, add the water, herbs and tomatoes and continue to cook until the veggies become slightly tender.

Chili Tofu Burger

Serves 4

Ingredients

2 teaspoons of extra virgin olive oil

½ teaspoon of organic salt or sea salt

6 teaspoons of organic chili sauce

100g onions

100g green bell pepper

500g of ground beef

Pepper

Directions

1. Begin by chopping the onions and bell peppers and then add oil in a pan. Then stir-fry the two ingredients for about 5 minutes.

2. In the pan, add in the beef and cook for 15 minutes or until cooked then add the salt, chili sauce and pepper and stir well.

3. If the dish is too dry, you can add in water and then serve the burger.

Wholegrain Mustard Crackers

Serves 15

Ingredients

2 1/2 tablespoons of coconut flour

1 tablespoon of wholegrain mustard

Pinch of salt

2 tablespoons sesame seeds

1 egg

1 tablespoon melted or coconut oil, or ghee

3 tablespoons tahini paste

Directions

1. Preheat your oven to 338 degrees F.

2. Now in a bowl, combine mustard, salt, sesame seeds, egg, coconut oil/ghee and tahini.

3. To this mixture, add in coconut flour and then combine until it thickens. In case you're not using coconut floor, add more flour since coconut is a moisture absorber.

4. Start rolling the mixture into a ball and then position the ball on a baking parchment paper

that is slightly greased. It should measure around 40cm by 40cm.

5. Using your hands, flatten it in the middle until you form a flat pancake; and then use a different parchment paper to cover.

6. Now flatten the pancake using a rolling pin until you make a 3-5mm thin dough layer. Start from the middle and roll the dough evenly in 4 directions.

7. At this point, make a small incision mark using a knife. Cut both vertically and horizontally to help the cracker break easily after cooking.

8. Now position the contents on the middle shelf of your oven and then cook for around 15 minutes.

9. Once the outer edges appear cooked, remove from heat and slice the edges off. Then cook for 3-5 more minutes, or until cooked through.

10. Put the cooked cracker layer to cool. Serve and enjoy.

Lamb Tagine with Onions and Tomatoes

Serves 4

Ingredients

1 tablespoon of sesame seeds, toasted

2 tablespoons of fresh cilantro, finely chopped

2 teaspoons of granulated sugar

2 tablespoons of fresh flat-leaf parsley, finely chopped

2 large red onions, 1 finely chopped

2 minced garlic cloves

1 28 oz. can of whole peeled tomatoes

½ teaspoon of turmeric, ground

2 ¾ lb. bone in leg of lamb steaks (3-5 pieces)

½ teaspoon ginger, ground

3 tablespoons extra-virgin olive oil

1 teaspoon cinnamon, grounded

Black pepper and kosher salt to taste

Directions

1. Mix together the cilantro, parsley, garlic, ginger, turmeric, ¼ teaspoon of cinnamon, ¾ teaspoon of salt, pepper to taste, and 2 tablespoons of water then add the olive oil and mix.

2. Then add the lamb steak to the marinade, one by one to coat each then cover and refrigerate for one hour. Remember to turn them occasionally.

3. As you wait, drain the tomatoes in a sieve. Using a paring knife, make a small incision and gently squeeze out all the seeds and juice then set this aside.

4. On the bottom of an 11-12 inch tagine, scatter the chopped onions. Then arrange the lamb in a snug and drizzle the rest of the marinade.

5. At this point, arrange the tomatoes (drained) around the lamb and sprinkle 1 teaspoon of sugar and ¼ teaspoon of cinnamon on the tomatoes.

6. Once done, cut the remaining onions crosswise into 1/8 inch coin rounds, and lay the un-separated onion rings on the lamb. Then sprinkle the remaining 1 teaspoon sugar and ½

teaspoon cinnamon before adding add a pinch of salt on onions.

7. Cook the Tagine uncovered for about fifteen minutes over medium heat, and be sure to nudge the lamb occasionally as doing so helps prevent sticking. Now cook until the onions are translucent.

8. Then add a ¼ cup of water around the edges making sure not to disturb the sugar and cinnamon.

9. Prop a wooden spoon between the base and the lid before covering, and then simmer gently on low heat. Cook until the lamb is very tender and the onions are soft; let's say in 2-2.5 hours.

10. Finally, drizzle some water from time to time to keep the sauce loose. If the sauce is too watery, remove the lid at the end of cooking. Garnish with sesame seeds and serve hot.

Green Chile Chicken Breasts with Sauce

Servings: 6

Ingredients

1 tablespoon sesame seeds, toasted

2 tablespoons whipping cream

1 tablespoon canola oil

6 chicken breast cutlets or fillets

3/4 teaspoon of salt, divided

1 clove garlic, thinly sliced

3 tablespoons slivered almonds, toasted

3 scallions, sliced, separated white and green parts

3/4 cup of fresh green chilies, chopped and seeded

1/2 cup chicken broth, reduced-sodium

2 cups almond milk, unsweetened

Directions

1. In a medium-sized saucepan, mix together green chilies, almond milk, garlic, scallion

whites, broth and ¼ teaspoon salt and bring the mixture to a boil.

2. Then minimize the heat and simmer for about 20-30 minutes, until the mixture is reduced by half.

3. Now puree the mixture in a blender or immersion blender until smooth.

4. Using the remaining ½ teaspoon of salt, season the chicken and then heat some oil over medium-heat in a large non-skillet.

5. In the skillet, cook half of the chicken for about 1-2 minutes each side, until browned.

6. Then put the first batch of the chicken in the pan and then pour the sauce. Cook at low heat to simmer, for about 4-7 minutes until the chicken is tender and cooked through.

7. When done, remove from heat and then pour the sauce over your chicken.

8. Use the reserved sesame seeds and scallion greens to sprinkle on top. Serve and enjoy.

Turkey Breast with Maple Mustard Glaze

Serves: 6

Ingredients

1 tablespoon of ghee

2 tablespoons Dijon mustard

¼ cup maple syrup

½ teaspoon black pepper, freshly ground

1 teaspoon salt

½ teaspoon smoked paprika

½ teaspoon dried sage

1 teaspoon dried thyme

5-pound whole turkey breast

2 teaspoons olive oil

Directions

1. To begin with, preheat your Air fryer to 350°F.

2. Then brush olive oil over the turkey breast to coat it.

3. Combine pepper, salt, paprika, sage and thyme and then rub the seasonings on the turkey breast.

4. Place the seasoned turkey breast to the basket of Air fryer and cook for 25 minutes on the pre-heated oven.

5. Flip over the breast and then fry the other side for about 12 minutes. Check whether the internal temperature has reached 165°F, which means the meat is fully cooked.

6. Meanwhile, mix together ghee, mustard and maple syrup in a small saucepan. After the turkey breast is cooked, turn it to an upright position and brush graze all over.

7. Then air fry for another 5 minutes until the skin is brown and crispy. Allow the turkey breast to cool when loosely covered with foil for about 5-10 minutes then slice and serve.

Paleo Fish Cakes

Serves 6

Ingredients

6 basil leaves

1 (6.5 ounce) can fresh shrimp, drained

1 tablespoon Italian seasoning

1/2 cup paleo-friendly bread crumbs

1 bunch fresh parsley

1 egg

6 ounces fresh bay scallops

5 sun-dried tomatoes, chopped

4 tablespoons almond flour

4 cloves garlic

4 tablespoons olive oils, divided

1/2 medium onion

2 fresh hot Chile peppers, seeded

1 (9-ounce) can tuna, drained

Directions

1. Heat a tablespoon of olive oil in a skillet, over medium heat and then stir in scallops.

2. Cook until they turn white on all sides. Drain and then set aside the scallops.

3. Put garlic, egg, 1 tablespoon olive oil, sundried tomatoes and onion in a food processor.

4. Add in Italian seasoning, basil leaves, parsley and chilies and pulse on medium setting to obtain a chopped consistency.

5. Now add in tuna, shrimp and scallops and pulse on low. Pour in breadcrumbs and continue to pulse to obtain a firm and sticky puree.

6. Form the puree into palm-size patties that measure 1 inch thick and set onto a plate. Cover and keep chilled for 1 hour.

7. In a large skillet, heat 2 tablespoons of olive oil over medium heat. Dust the patties lightly in the flour as you shake off any excess.

8. Put the patties in the skillet and cook on both sides until golden brown.

Paleo Snack Recipes

Roasted Brussels sprouts With Bacon

Serves 4

Ingredients

1 tablespoon of maple syrup

1/4 cup pomegranate seeds

3 slices hickory-smoked bacon

Pepper

Salt

2 tablespoons of better body foods omega oil

2 large apples roughly chopped

1 lb. Brussels sprouts, halved length-wise

Directions

1. Begin by pre-heating the oven to 400 degrees F.

2. Then toss together apples, sprouts and oils in a large bowl until well blended.

3. In a big-rimmed baking sheet, spread the blended mixture taking care not to crowd the

sprouts. Season the mixture with pepper and salt.

4. Bake the sprouts for about 15 minutes, stir briefly and then bake until lightly browned, or for 10 to 15 minutes.

5. Meanwhile, heat a frying pan to medium heat and then cook the bacon until crispy and golden brown, flipping once.

6. Now move the meat to a towel-lined bowl and drain out any excess oil. Move the cooked Brussels sprouts to a large bowl.

7. Finally crumble the bacon and now add in maple syrup and pomegranate seeds. Toss to mix and then serve.

Paleo Egg Cups

Serves: 12

Ingredients

8 asparagus spears, chopped

12 strips uncured organic bacon, cooked

12 eggs

Coconut oil or ghee

Black pepper

Sea Salt

Directions

1. Heat the oven to 400 degrees F. Meanwhile, grease about 12 cups of a muffin pan.

2. Then lay a bacon strip in each cup, and push it down so that it doesn't hang outside.

3. Crack an egg in each muffin cup and distribute the asparagus in each. Add some salt and pepper then bake in the middle of the oven for about 15 minutes.

4. Serve the eggs warm or keep cooled until ready to serve.

Soy-Free Beef Jerky

Serves 4-6

Ingredients

2-inch piece fresh ginger, thinly sliced

2 tablespoons salt

2 tablespoons gluten-free liquid smoke

1/4 cup coconut sugar

1/4 cup apple cider vinegar

1/2 cup coconut aminos

2.5 pounds very lean beef, trimmed of all fat

Directions

1. In a large zip-top bag or glass container that has a tight-fitting lid, mix together ginger, salt, liquid smoke, sugar, apple cider vinegar and coconut aminos.

2. Close the container and shake until most of the salt and sugar has dissolved, and then set aside.

3. Slice the beef then add it to the brine, seal and toss. Keep it chilled for around 8 hours, turning it twice.

4. Now preheat your dehydrator to about 165 degrees F or higher. Drain of the brine then discard ginger. Carefully arrange the strips of beef on the dehydrator trays.

5. To test if the beef jerky is ready, simply allow strips of beef to cool down at room temperature then bent it. The jerky should be firm and not flexible, yet should crack not bend. In case it doesn't crack, return it to the dehydrator.

6. Store the beef jerky in the fridge up to a week or just an airtight container. To make an easy to chew jerky, slice it rump roast, flank steak or a round steak about 1 inch wide by 4-inch long and 1/8th inch thick strips.

Garlic Lemon Chicken Skewers

Serves 8

Ingredients

2 tablespoons fresh parsley, chopped

3/4 cup Tessemae's lemon garlic

4 chicken breasts, cut into 1 inch cubes

Directions

1. To a bowl or zip lock bag, add the lemon garlic dressing and chicken and let coat for a few minutes. Keep it chilled for 1 to 3 hours.

2. Meanwhile, preheat the grill to around 500 degrees and then start treading the chicken onto the skewers. If using wooden skewers, soak them in water about 30 minutes before use.

3. Once the grill is hot enough, put the skewers on the grill and cook until the chicken is well cooked, while flipping halfway through to facilitate even cook.

4. After about 15 minutes or so, remove from the grill and garnish with fresh herbs such as parsley or others. You can also cook the chicken under a broiler or a grill pan and

ensure the internal temperature reaches 160 degrees before serving.

Roasted Beet Dip

Serves: 2 cups

Ingredients

1/3 cup of loosely packed cilantro leaves, finely chopped

2 teaspoons fresh lemon juice

2 teaspoons green chile, chopped

2 teaspoons minced garlic

3/4 teaspoon coriander seeds

3/4 teaspoon cumin seeds

1/2 teaspoon Celtic sea salt

1/4 cup extra-virgin olive oil

4 cups peeled and cubed raw beets

Directions

1. Preheat your oven to 400 degrees F. Meanwhile, line a baking sheet with parchment paper or silicon liner.

2. Toss the beets with ¼ teaspoons of salt and 2 tablespoons. Then layer the beets on the baking sheet and roast for 1 hour. Toss occasionally, until the beets are tender.

3. In a heavy skillet, heat coriander and cumin over medium high heat for about 2 minutes, while stirring. Do not burn them, as they could develop bitterness.

4. Crush the seeds with a mortar and pestle or grind in a spice grinder. Put the beets in a food processor and add in 2 tablespoons of oil, ¼ teaspoon salt, lemon juice, chile, garlic and the toasted and ground seeds.

5. Blast until fully incorporated then adjust the salt, lemon, chile and garlic to taste. Move the dip to a bowl and add in cilantro. Stir to mix and serve with any of the chips or crackers in the book.

Spicy Tomato Recipe

Serves: 1

Ingredients

1/2 cup ice

Lemon squeeze

1 teaspoon hot sauce or black pepper to taste

1/3 cup frozen spinach or small handful raw spinach

1/2 avocado

1/4 cup chopped cucumber

1/2 cup chopped tomato

Directions

1. In a large plate, place the above ingredients and toss to combine.

2. Spray black pepper to taste and then serve with any of the crips, skewers or crackers in the book.

Chicken Salad Stuffed Tomatoes

Serves 6

Ingredients

4 tablespoons ranch dip

4 tablespoons buffalo wing sauce

1 carrot, peeled and shredded

3 tablespoons of minced red onion

2-3 stalks celery, finely chopped

1 lb. cooked chicken meat, chopped or shredded

2 lbs. small tomatoes

Salt and pepper

For Dairy-free ranch dip

Serves 1/4 cup

Salt and pepper

Pinch paprika

1/8 teaspoon garlic powder

1 teaspoon of dried dill

1 tablespoon of scallion greens or French minced chives

1 tablespoon fresh parsley, minced

1 teaspoon lemon juice

4 tablespoons mayo

Directions

1. In a large mixing bowl, mix together the ranch dip and the wing sauce until blended.

2. Then add in the rest of the ingredients apart from the tomatoes until fully mixed. Taste and season the mixture as you like.

3. Now cut a slice off the stem from each tomato end and scoop out the insides. Using the chicken salad, fill the tomato spaces as you press using the back of the spoon.

4. Serve the stuffed tomatoes with the wing sauce and enjoy. To make the dairy-free ranch dip, simply mix all the ingredients and keep it chilled until ready to serve.

Blueberry Coconut Popsicles

Serves: 10

Ingredients

2-3 tablespoons of pure maple syrup

3 cups fresh blueberries

1 can full-fat coconut milk

Directions

1. To a blender, add maple syrup, blueberries and coconut milk then process until smooth. Scrap down the sides of the food processor as required.

2. Move the mixture into a Popsicle mould leaving around ¼ inch space at the top of the mold to help the popsicles expand in the freezer.

3. Follow the mold directions to insert the Popsicle sticks in the mold. Freeze the popsicle for about 6 to 8 hours.

4. Once hard enough, remove from the freezer and then let thaw for 1-2 minutes. You can run the mold lukewarm water to loosen the popsicles if need be.

5. Put the popsicle mold on flat surface and gently wiggle the snack out. Serve!

Paleo Energy Bars

Serves 5 bars

Ingredients

1/2 cup almond flour

2 tablespoons of arrowroot starch

1/4 cup vanilla protein powder

1/4 cup seeds

1/3 cup dried fruit

1/4 cup nuts

1 medium banana

Directions

1. Using a fork, mash the banana in a medium bowl then add in almond flour and arrowroot starch. Mix to blend.

2. Add in your other preferred mix-ins and now grease a small pan to pour the mixture in. Spread the mixture and press it down to evenly distribute it.

3. Bake the dough at 275 degrees F until the edges start browning or for about 30 to 40 minutes.

4. Once done, remove from the oven and cut into squares or bars and then serve.

Rosemary Sweet Potato Chips

Serves 10

Ingredients

Salt & pepper to taste

2 sweet potatoes

2 tablespoons of coconut oil

Directions

1. First, preheat your oven to 400 degrees F.

2. Using a sharp knife, slice your sweet potatoes to bite-sizes and then toss together with coconut oil. Ensure you rub the sweet potatoes fully in oil to coat.

3. Now using a parchment paper, line your baking sheet and then arrange your sweet potatoes on it.

4. Add salt, pepper and rosemary to season and bake in the preheated oven for 25-30 minutes. To ensure they bake well with crispier texture, flip the potatoes once.

5. Once crispy brown with soft centers, remove from heat and let them cool to harden.

Blueberry Chia Jam Bars

Serves: 16

Ingredients

1 teaspoon of vanilla or almond extract

1/4 cup water

1/4 cup maple syrup

1 tablespoon chia seeds

1 1/2 cups gluten-free rolled buckwheat

1 1/2 cups raw almonds

For Blueberry layer

2 tablespoons of maple syrup

1/3 cup + 1 tablespoon chia seeds

12 oz. blueberries, fresh or frozen

Topping

1/3 cup maple syrup

1/3 cup coconut oil

1/3 cup cacao powder

Directions

1. Using unbleached parchment paper, line a 9 by 5 inch loaf pan and set aside. Put the main ingredients in a blender and pulse to combine.

2. Press the mixture evenly into the parchment-lined pan using a spatula. Process the blueberries in a blender or food processor.

3. Add in chia seeds and puree to blend. Allow the mixture to sit until it thickens, for about 20 minutes. Then spread it over the loaf ingredients.

4. Mix the topping ingredients in a small bowl and pour over the chia jam blueberry layer. Spread the topping evenly.

5. Now freeze to bars until firm then let thaw for 15-20 minutes at room temperature. Cut and serve or store the bars for up to a week in the fridge.

Air-fried Pork and Pumpkin Empanadas

Serves: 10

Ingredients

Olive oil

1 package of 10 empanada discs, thawed

Black pepper, freshly ground

1 teaspoon salt

½ teaspoon dried thyme

½ teaspoon cinnamon

1 red chili pepper, minced

3 tablespoons water

1½ cups pumpkin purée

½ onion, diced

1 pound ground pork

2 tablespoons olive oil

Directions

1. Pre-heat the air fryer to 370°F.

2. Then over medium heat, pre-heat a medium sauté pan. Add in onions and the pork and sauté the ingredients for 5 minutes.

3. Once the onion softens and the pork has browned, drain the fat from the pan and discard.

3. Now add in red chili pepper, water, pumpkin puree, salt, thyme, cinnamon and pepper to the pork mixture.

4. Stir to combine the ingredients then simmer the mixture for about 10 minutes. Now remove from the pan and let it cool down.

5. Put the empanada onto a flat surface then brush its edges using water. In the center of each disk, put 2-3 tablespoons of the filing and fold the dough over the fillings. Make a half moon shape.

6. Using a tip of a fork, crimp its edges shut and then use olive oil to brush both sides of the empanadas.

7. Now place a few pieces of empanadas in the Air fryer basket and cook for about 14 minutes. Turn it over after 8 minutes.

8. Serve warm and enjoy.

Paleo Raw French Fries

Serves 6

Ingredients

1 teaspoon of sea salt

2 teaspoons curcumin

1/2 cups olive or hemp seed oil, cold pressed

4 kohlrabies cabbage

For Ketchup:

1/2 cup pure water

1 squeeze lemon juice

5 dates

3 pieces sun dried tomatoes

3 tomatoes

Directions

1. Begin by cutting the kohlrabies cabbage like French fries and then put in a bowl.

2. Put some salt, curcumin and oil in a bowl and combine; and then pour this mixture over your fries.

3. Allow the mixture to cool for around 10 minutes, and then drain.

4. Scoop the mixture into paper towels to remove any excess oil.

5. To prepare the ketchup, place the ingredients into a powerful blender starting with water, lemon juice and tomatoes. Put the dried tomatoes and the dates on top and blend completely.

Crispy Kale Chips

Servings: 8

Ingredients

2 tablespoons filtered water

½ teaspoon gray sea salt or pink rock salt

1 tablespoon raw honey

2 tablespoons nutritional yeast

1 lemon, juiced

1 cup sweet potato, grated

1 cup fresh cashews, soaked 2 hours

2 bunches green curly kales, cut into bite sizes

Directions

1. In a food processor or blender, process all the ingredients apart from kales until smooth.

2. Put kales in a large mixing bowl and then pour over the blended ingredients. Combine fully with your hands so that you coat the kale.

3. Transfer the kale onto unbleached parchment paper, and then set the oven to 150 degrees to dehydrate the kales for 2 hours.

4. Turn the leaves at some point to ensure smooth drying. Once done, remove from the oven and keep in an airtight container.

Toasted Almonds

Serves: 4

Ingredients

1 cup raw almonds

1 tablespoon fresh rosemary, chopped; optional:

Directions

1. In a dry sauté pan, toast the almonds over medium heat.

2. Cook the almonds until fragrant.

3. Once ready, remove from heat. Store in an airtight container.

Pickled Brussels sprouts

Yields: 40

Ingredients

5 cups of water

5 cloves of garlic, halved

1 1/4 teaspoon of hot pepper flakes

5 cups of white vinegar

7 tablespoons pickling salt

2 pounds of Brussels sprouts

5 1-pint canning jars with lids and rings

Directions

1. Soak the sprouts in a bowl of salted water for around 15 minutes and then drain well. Sanitize your mason jars beforehand and set the lids and rings in boiling water.

2. Now combine the water, salt and vinegar in a large stockpot, and bring to a boil while stirring frequently to dissolve the salt.

3. At this point, pack one head of dill or dill seeds, half garlic clove and a half teaspoon of hot pepper flakes (if using) in each mason jar.

Add the Brussels sprouts into individual jars but leave about ½ an inch of headspace.

4. Fill the hot liquid into the jars and ensure to leave headspace of about ½ inch.

6. Remove any air bubbles, adjusting the headspace when necessary, and then wipe off any spilled liquid from the jars. Set the lids and tighten with the rings.

7. At this point, place the jars inside a hot water bath canner and process for 10 minutes in the hot, boiling water.

8. Finally remove and set aside to cool completely for 12 to 24 hours. It's advisable to store in a dark place and wait for at least 21 days before serving.

Vanilla Pumpkin Seed Clusters

Yields: 30

Ingredients

2 teaspoons coconut sugar

2 teaspoons honey

1 teaspoon vanilla extract

½ cup pumpkin seeds

Water, boiled

Directions

1. Preheat the oven to 150 degrees Celsius, as you combine vanilla, coconut sugar and honey in a small bowl.

2. Add in a drop of boiled water; to create runny syrup. Pour in the pumpkin seeds and stir to evenly coat the seeds.

3. Dollop a teaspoon of pumpkin seeds onto a baking sheet, and repeat this until all seeds are on the baking sheet.

4. Cook for about 15-20 minutes to brown the seeds. Remove from the oven and cool for some time.

5. After cooling, press the clusters together to ensure they don't fall apart, will dry quickly. Serve once cool and dry.

Pizza Crust

Serves 1

Ingredients

50g sun dried tomatoes

Pinch of pepper

4 tablespoons extra-virgin olive oil, cold-pressed

100g flax seeds

200g sunflower seeds

Pinch of organic salt or sea salt

Wild garlic (ramson), fresh

Preferred paleo spices

Directions

1. Pre-soak the sunflower seeds for more than 4 hours or overnight.

2. Add in flax seeds into a mixer, and grind them to obtained fine-grained powder.

3. Remove the sunflower seeds from the water and blend them in the mixer for a few seconds.

4. Transfer these to a bowl and knead the dough using your fingers to get the desired consistency. You can also add in some olive oil or distilled water.

5. Now create a few pizza breads or pizza crusts and place them in a dehydrator overnight or at least 12 hours. Alternatively, an oven can save the day in case you don't have a dehydrator.

6. Choose your preferred paleo topping, cook and then serve the pizza.

Brownie Bites

Servings 8

Ingredients

1/3 cup brewed coffee or water

2 teaspoons pure vanilla extract

1/2 cup coconut oil melted

1/2 cup full-fat coconut milk, unsweetened

2 eggs

1 teaspoon salt

2 teaspoons baking soda

2 teaspoons baking powder

3/4 cup cocoa powder, unsweetened

1 cup coconut sugar

2 cups almond flour, blanched

Directions

1. Use coconut oil to grease the slow cooker.

2. Mix all ingredients and spread them evenly in the slow cooker.

3. Cook the mixture for 4-5 hours until well cooked through.

4. At this point, allow to cool for 30 minutes then scoop out using a large spoon or cookie scoop. Make it into balls.

5. Drizzle caramel glaze if you like.

Coconut Cupcakes

Serves 8

Ingredients

20 grams dark chocolate, 85% cocoa

2 tablespoons psyllium husk

4 tablespoons coconut oil

2000ml coconut milk, unsweetened

90g coconut flakes, unsweetened

120g vanilla-flavored protein powder

Directions

1. Combine the protein powder with psylium and coconut flakes in a medium sized bowl.

2. Add in coconut oil and coconut milk into the dry ingredients and stir to incorporate.

3. Sub-divide the batter into cupcake forms to fill 7 stand size cupcake forms. You can use paper cupcake forms or silicon molds.

4. Grind and melt the chocolate, and apply onto the cupcakes.

5. At this point, put the cupcakes in a freezer for ½ an hour, to firm them up.

6. Once hardened to your liking, remove the cupcakes from the freezer and keep in the fridge.

Paleo Desserts

Beet Chocolate Pudding

Serves: 4

Ingredients

1/8 teaspoon sea salt

1/2 teaspoon of cinnamon, ground

1/3 cup pure maple syrup

1/2 cup full fat canned coconut milk

1/2 cup red beet roasted

1/2 cup of unsweetened cocoa powder

2 large ripe avocados, peeled and diced

Directions

1. Add all the ingredients into a food processor and process until smooth.

2. At some point while processing, stop the processor a couple of times to scrap the sides then re-start again to get a smoother consistency.

3. Move the pudding to a sealable container and keep it chilled for a few hours. Serve it with coconut whipped cream.

Coffee Ice Cream

Serves: 8

Ingredients

¼ teaspoon stevia extract

1 teaspoon organic vanilla extract

2 tablespoons raw coconut nectar

1 cup organic coffee, double strength

1/4 teaspoon sea salt

2 teaspoons gelatin, unflavored

48 tablespoons organic coconut milk

1 oz. Kahlua

Directions

1. Add the organic coffee to a medium saucepan, and then simmer to reduce the amount to ½ cup.

2. Sprinkle gelatin on the coffee and then warm it over low heat, until the gelatin fully dissolves. You don't need to stir.

3. Spoon your coffee mixture into a blender, then blend until smooth. Add the coconut

nectar, stevia and sea salt and continue to blend.

4. Add the vanilla, milk and Kahlua and continue to blend. Once done, pour in a glass container and cool for 6 hours while covered to get a custard-like substance.

5. Transfer to your ice cream maker and follow the manufacturer's instructions to make ice cream. Freeze for about 2 hours until it is firm.

Banana Brownies

Yields 16

Ingredients

A little ghee

1/2 cup semi-sweet dark chocolate chips

1/2 cup walnuts

1½ cups rice flour

½ teaspoon baking powder

2 tablespoons cocoa powder, unsweetened

1 ounce soy protein powder or chocolate whey

1/2 cup almond milk

2 teaspoons vanilla extract

3/4 cup coconut sugar

1/4 cup sunflower oil

1 egg

1 cup ripe bananas, mashed; thawed, frozen

Directions

1. Use ghee to grease a baking pan or a 9×9 glass casserole dish as you preheat the oven to 350 degrees F.

2. Mix together the egg and mashed banana in a large bowl and then add in milk, vanilla, sugar and oil.

3. Also mix together baking powder, cocoa and milk protein powder in a small bowl and then blend in the dry mixture into the wet ingredients.

4. Stir in the flour, chocolate chips and walnuts until fully blended.

5. Pour the batter into a pan or dish, and bake in the preheated oven for 25-30 minutes. Once ready, cool in a pan and then cut into squares to serve.

Vanilla Chia Pudding

Serves: 2

Ingredients

1 teaspoon vanilla liquid stevia

1 teaspoon vanilla extract

1/3 cup chia seeds

1 cup almond milk, unsweetened

Dairy-free whipped cream, optional

Directions

1. Combine and whisk the ingredients together and then pour into serving glasses.

2. Keep in the fridge for 10 minutes until set

3. If desired, top with some whipped cream and enjoy.

Banana Pecan Ice Cream

Serves 4

Ingredients

1/2 cup pecans, chopped & toasted

1/2 cup canned coconut milk, chilled

3 tablespoons ghee

4 bananas

Directions

1. Slice 2 bananas and then put the slices into a sealed bag in the freezer for around 8 hours or precisely overnight

2. Also slice the 2 remaining bananas into rounds that are ½ an inch thick.

3. In a sauté pan, melt the ghee over medium or high heat.

4. Put the banana slices in the sauté pan and cook the mixture until the bananas turn golden brown. Flip the slices to make sure the other side has browned.

5. In a thick Ziploc bag or another container, pour the caramelized bananas and keep in the freezer for 8 hours or overnight.

6. Put all the 4 frozen bananas in a high speed blender. Include both the caramelized and the un-caramelized bananas.

7. Pulse the frozen bananas to have them begin to appear like large bread crumbs, and then add in the coconut milk and blend well. Keep scrapping down the sides and pressing the banana crumbles down to the center a number of times.

8. Blend until a smooth mixture is formed, of thick soft-serve ice cream consistency.

9. Add in the pecans to your ice cream and combine using a rubber spatula.

10. Once done, scoop into bowls and serve.

Pineapple Ice Cream

Serves: 6

Ingredients

3 ¼ tablespoon activated black charcoal

Small pinch of salt

1 teaspoon coconut extract

1 teaspoon vanilla extract

¾ cup coconut sugar

½ cup almond milk

1 cup crushed pineapple

1 cup raw cashews, soaked 2 days and rinsed

2 cups full fat coconut milk, chilled

Directions

1. Mix together almond milk and cashews in a high-speed blender and blend to obtain a thick and creamy consistency.

2. Add in the rest of the ingredients apart from the pineapple and puree until smooth.

3. Transfer the ice cream to a bowl, whisk in pineapple and mix well. Add the mixture to the

ice cream maker and follow the manufacturer's instructions to churn.

4. As soon as you obtain creamy frozen ice cream, serve or alternatively store in an airtight container. Keep it chilled for at least 2 hours to freeze fully.

Fried Banana

Serves 1

Ingredients

Olive oil or coconut oil

A pinch of cinnamon

1 tablespoon organic honey

1 banana, sliced

Directions

1. In a skillet, over medium heat, lightly drizzle the oil.

2. Arrange your banana slices in the skillet and cook for around 1-2 minutes on both sides.

3. As the banana slices cook, whisk a tablespoon of water and organic honey.

4. Remove the pan from heat and pour in your honey mixture over the sliced cooked bananas.

4. Once cool, sprinkle with cinnamon and serve.

Key Lime Pie

Serves 12

Ingredients

For filling

2/3 cup lime juice

1 cup coconut oil

6 tablespoons organic honey

6 avocados

For Crust

1/4 cup coconut flour

1/4 cup coconut, shredded, unsweetened

2 tablespoons honey

2 tablespoons almond butter

1/2 cup dates

1 1/2 cups almond flour/meal

Directions

1. Put the crust ingredients in a food processor, and then pulse until it turns grainy. The pulsed contents should appear sticky when pressed,

but should not form a ball on themselves. In case it does, add in almond flour.

2. To form a crust, dump the blended ingredients into a spring form pan and then press down.

3. Wipe out your processor and then put the filling ingredients in it. Start to blend the mixture for around 4-5 minutes to form a smooth mixture.

4. Now pour over the crust and then smooth out. Put the pie in a freezer, for 2 hours and then serve when cool.

Pumpkin Chocolate Chip Cookies

Yields 16

Ingredients

3/4 cup chocolate chips

½ teaspoon vanilla

1 tablespoon coconut oil

2 tablespoons honey

2 tablespoons applesauce

¼ cup pumpkin puree or canned

1 free-range egg

½ teaspoon baking powder

½ teaspoon baking soda

½ teaspoon sea salt

1 ½ teaspoons pumpkin pie spice

1/3 cup tapioca flour

1 cup almond flour

Directions

1. Preheat the oven to around 350 degrees F. Then use a non-stick parchment paper to line your baking sheet.

2. Whisk together baking powder, baking soda, sea salt, pumpkin pie spice, tapioca flour and almond flour in a mixing bowl.

3. Also whisk together vanilla, oil, honey, applesauce, pumpkin puree and egg in a separate mixing bowl until smooth and well blended.

4. Now pour the wet mixture into the bowl with the dry ingredients, and continue to whisk to mix.

5. At this point, add in chocolate chips and continue to mix until blended.

6. Scoop around 2 tablespoons of dough and place on the baking sheet, 2 inches.

7. Bake in the preheated oven for around 8-9 minutes and then store in an airtight container .The cookies are best served the same day.

Chocolate Chia Raspberry Cobblers

Serves: 6

Ingredients

2 1/2 oz. pitted dates, chopped

2 cups raspberries, fresh

2 teaspoons pure vanilla extract

3 tablespoons pure maple syrup

3 tablespoons cocoa powder, unsweetened

1/2 cup chia seeds

1½ cups almond or rice milk

1/2 cup rolled buckwheat

1 1/4 oz. raw hazelnuts, unsalted

Directions

1. Preheat the oven to 375 degrees F and then line a baking sheet using parchment paper.

2. Put buckwheat and hazelnuts onto the baking sheet and bake for about 12 minutes. Once the hazelnut become fragrant and the buckwheat are lightly toasted, remove from the oven.

3. Whisk together vanilla, maple syrup, cocoa powder, chia seeds and milk in a large bowl for 2 minutes. Set aside for 10 minutes to form a thick pudding-like substance.

4. Layer the chocolate-chia seed mixture, dates, raspberries, hazelnuts and buckwheat in 6 mason jars.

5. Keep the mixture in the fridge for up to 3 days until ready to serve.

Almond Flour Buns

Serves 10

Ingredients

1 tablespoon liquid sweetener

60g cooking cream, about 35% fat

Pinch of salt

1 teaspoon baking powder

1 tablespoon ground flaxseed

2 tablespoons goji berries, dried and ground

3 tablespoons almond flour

1 tablespoon walnut oil

4 tablespoons grape seed oil

4 eggs

30g ghee

Directions

1. Preheat your oven to 350 degrees F.

2. Using an electric mixer, beat eggs well in a medium or large bowl and then blend oil into the eggs, gradually adding a tablespoon and

continue to whisk. You can use other alternatives for walnut oil and the grape seed.

3. Once done, blend the cream into the mixture, adding a tablespoon a little by a little; whisking until fully incorporated.

4. Now add in some warm melted ghee into the mixture, and combine with the rest of the ingredients, before adding the liquid sweetener.

5. Add in the mixed dry ingredients comprising of salt, baking powder, flaxseed, goji beans and almond flour to the cream batter. You just need to add a tablespoon each time, as you gently mix by hand.

6. Once done, transfer the dough to a non-stick bun tray, which has capacity to hold from 10-12 cups, based on the size of your buns.

7. Bake for around 15 minutes, up until the buns turn golden. After removing the baked buns from the oven, they will deflate slightly.

8. At this point serve the cups when hot, and then store the remaining buns in the fridge if you like.

With all we've learned in mind, here is a 30 day meal plan that you can follow to help you get closer to attaining all the benefits we discussed. As you will notice, the meal plan does not have snacks and desserts. That's on purpose. You want to make sure that the amount of energy that you end up consuming doesn't end up becoming too much such that your body gets into a fat accumulation mode as opposed to a fat burning mode. You can start introducing snacks and desserts intermittently after the 30 days- keep in mind that the diet is something you should follow the rest of your life and not just for a few days.

30 Day Mean Plan

Day 1

Breakfast: Paleo meat bagel

Lunch: Paleo Copycat Zuppa Toscana

Dinner: Tex-Mex Turkey Skillet

Day 2

Breakfast: Paleo meat bagel

Lunch: Paleo Copycat Zuppa Toscana

Dinner: Paleo Pineapple Fried Rice

Day 3

Breakfast: Gooey Paleo Cinnamon Rolls

Lunch: Curried Tuna-Chia Salad

Dinner: Paleo Pizza Chicken

Day 4

Breakfast: Paleo Blueberry Muffin

Lunch: Spicy Cashew Chicken Soup

Dinner: Lebanese Lemon Chicken

Day 5

Breakfast: Banana Bread French Toast

Lunch: Almond and Sesame Asparagus Salad

Dinner: Chorizo & Vegetable Stew

Day 6

Breakfast: Gooey Paleo Cinnamon Rolls

Lunch: Turkish Lamb Kebab Koftas

Dinner: Chicken with Fig and Shallot Compote

Day 7

Breakfast: Rhubarb, Apple and Ginger Muffin

Lunch: Fresh Tomatoes with Basil

Dinner: Paleo Mini Meatloaves

Day 8

Breakfast: Apricot Power Bars

Lunch: Citrusy Shaved Zucchini & Sardine Salad

Dinner: Grilled Chicken Satay

Day 9

Breakfast: Coffee Coconut Frappuccino

Lunch: Basil Spinach Salad

Dinner: Ground Beef Stroganoff

Day 10

Breakfast: Buckwheat and Quinoa Granola

Lunch: Kale Caesar Salad with Cherry Tomatoes

Dinner: Lamb Sliders with Ginger Cilantro Aioli

Day 11

Breakfast: Charred Cauliflower with Peppers and Almonds

Lunch: Prosciutto Melon Wrap-Ups

Dinner: Crab and Avocado Salad

Day 12

Breakfast: Loaf of Bread & Turmeric Bulletproof Energy Tea

Lunch: Slow Cooker Beef Minestrone

Dinner: Cod with Olives and Lemon

Day 13

Breakfast: Banana-Nut Paleo Pancakes

Lunch: Turkey Carrot Quiche

Dinner: Pumpkin Ratatouille

Day 14

Breakfast: Easy Breakfast Casserole

Lunch: Creepy Green Soup

Dinner: Chili Tofu Burger

Day 15

Breakfast: Raw Mixed Berry Yoghurt Tarts

Lunch: Chili-Beef Kebabs

Dinner: Wholegrain Mustard Crackers

Day 16

Breakfast: Paleo Kitchen Pumpkin Waffles

Lunch: Green Noodle Salad

Dinner: Lamb Tagine with Onions and Tomatoes

Day 17

Breakfast: Crockpot Breakfast Pie

Lunch: Turkey Bacon and Sweet Potato Hash

Dinner: Green Chile Chicken Breasts with Sauce

Day 18

Breakfast: Sausage and Asparagus Casserole

Lunch: Beet the Detox Salad

Dinner: Turkey Breast with Maple Mustard Glaze

Day 19

Breakfast: Avocado Canadian bacon and Egg Salad

Lunch: Pesto Zucchini Noodles

Dinner: Paleo Fish Cakes

Day 20

Breakfast: Nutty Breakfast

Lunch: Turkey Carrot Quiche

Dinner: Paleo Fish Cakes

Day 21

Breakfast: Avocado Canadian bacon and Egg Salad

Lunch: Slow Cooker Beef Minestrone

Dinner: Green Chile Chicken Breasts with Sauce

Day 22

Breakfast: Nutty Breakfast

Lunch: Prosciutto Melon Wrap-Ups

Dinner: Lamb Tagine with Onions and Tomatoes

Day 23

Breakfast: Easy Breakfast Casserole

Lunch: Green Noodle Salad

Dinner: Turkey Breast with Maple Mustard Glaze

Day 24

Breakfast: Paleo Kitchen Pumpkin Waffles

Lunch: Citrusy Shaved Zucchini & Sardine Salad

Dinner: Paleo Pineapple Fried Rice

Day 25

Breakfast: Banana Bread French Toast

Lunch: Chili-Beef Kebabs

Dinner: Tex-Mex Turkey Skillet

Day 26

Breakfast: Gooey Paleo Cinnamon Rolls

Lunch: Pesto Zucchini Noodles

Dinner: Lamb Tagine with Onions and Tomatoes

Day 27

Breakfast: Buckwheat and Quinoa Granola

Lunch: Turkey Carrot Quiche

Dinner: Paleo Mini Meatloaves

Day 28

Breakfast: Rhubarb, Apple and Ginger Muffin

Lunch: Turkish Lamb Kebab Koftas

Dinner: Paleo Pizza Chicken

Day 29

Breakfast: Apricot Power Bars

Lunch: Kale Caesar Salad with Cherry Tomatoes

Dinner: Grilled Chicken Satay

Day 30

Breakfast: Paleo Blueberry Muffin

Lunch: Basil Spinach Salad

Dinner: Cod with Olives and Lemon

Finally, for your reference, next, I will give links to some of the studies mentioned in this book.

Links To Studies Mentioned In The Book

http://ispub.com/IJNW/4/2/8738

https://www.ncbi.nlm.nih.gov/pubmed/17583796

https://www.ncbi.nlm.nih.gov/books/NBK535 50/

https://www.8weeksout.com/2011/09/21/fish-oil-build-muscle/

https://www.ncbi.nlm.nih.gov/pubmed/11255140

https://www.ncbi.nlm.nih.gov/pubmed/19209185

Conclusion

We have come to the end of the book. Thank you for reading and congratulations for reading until the end.

I truly hope you found the book educative and easy to follow. It is now time to put into practice what you've already learned and in no time, you're highly likely to succeed with the diet.

If you found the book valuable, can you recommend it to others? One way to do that is to post a review on Amazon.

Click here to leave a review for this book on Amazon!

https://amzn.to/2LLwsac

Thank you and good luck!

Check Out Our Other Books

Below you'll find some of our other books that are popular on Amazon and Kindle as well.

Go to the link below

ladypannana.com/amazonauthor

If the links do not work, for whatever reason, you can simply search for these titles on the Amazon website to find them.

Get Our 2 Audio Books for FREE!

Start Your Audible 30-day free trial and get these 2 Absolutely books:

Mediterranean Diet: Mediterranean Cookbook For Beginners, Lose Weight And Get Healthy

ladypannana.com/audiobook

Paleo Diet: Paleo Diet For Beginners, Lose Weight And Get Healthy

ladypannana.com/audiobooks

Check Out Our Other Books on
Amazon

The Mediterranean: Mediterranean Diet for Beginners to Rapid Weight Loss

ladypannana.com/books/mediterranean2

Ketogenic diet- Ketogenic Crock Pot Cookbook: Easy and Healthy Ketogenic Diet Recipes for Your Slow Cooker

ladypannana.com/books/crockpot

Instant Pot Cookbook: Quick and Easy
Traditional Indian Recipes for Everyday Eating

ladypannana.com/books/instantpot2

Paleo Diet: Paleo for Beginners for Rapid Weight Loss: Lose Up to 30 Pounds in 30 Days

ladypannana.com/books/paleo2

Vegan Slow Cooker Cookbook: Amazing Vegan Diet Recipes for your Entire Family

ladypannana.com/books/veganslowcooker

Low-Carb Cookbook: Simple and Healthy Low-Carb Recipes for the Entire Family

ladypannana.com/books/lowcarb

Plant-Based Diet: 4-Week Plant-Based Meal Plan to Get Maximum Benefits from Your Body

ladypannana.com/books/plantbaseddiet

Mediterranean Diet: Mediterranean Cookbook For Beginners, Lose Weight And Get Healthy

ladypannana.com/books/mediterranean1

Paleo Diet: Paleo Diet For Beginners, Lose Weight And Get Healthy

ladypannana.com/books/paleo1

Intermittent Fasting: The Easiest Way to Eat Whatever You Want, Burn Fat and Build Muscle

ladypannana.com/books/intermittent

PALEO DIET: 100 PALEO RECIPES FOR BEGINNERS TO LOSE WEIGHT AND GET HEALTHY

ladypannana.com/books/paleocookbook

Ketogenic Diet: The Complete Step-by-Step Guide for Beginners to Lose Weight and Get Healthy

ladypannana.com/books/ketodiet

Paleo Diet: Paleo Diet For Beginners, Lose Weight And Get Healthy

This book has actionable information on how to lose weight and get healthy by following the Paleo diet.

We can all agree that while there are major scientific breakthroughs on various facets of human life, the general population is struggling with some things that they really shouldn't be struggling with. For instance, obesity seems to be a worldwide problem and if the statistics are anything to go by, more and more people seem to be becoming obese or overweight.

Why is that so? Can't we just eat the right foods and avoid the wrong foods?

Well, while there are many theories behind that, there is a striking correlation between obesity and economic development. More precisely, developed nations seem to be struggling more than those that are still developing. What could be the problem? What's wrong with economic development and industrialization?

Simple: what the masses are consuming. With economic development comes more reliance on store bought ingredients and foods. What you may not know is that these ingredients have gone through genetic engineering, processing and much, much more that changes the original (natural ingredient) to some extent. This is bad for your body as these foods tend to have traces of substances that the body is not yet fully evolved to metabolize effectively. While the body does its best to metabolize some of these, most times the process is not efficient and it leaves behind toxic waste that is harmful for the body in the long term. The accumulation of this toxic waste in the body is what often times causes inflammation and fat accumulation (especially around the belly area). This perhaps explains why our modern society is plagued with so many diseases.

To reverse this toxic buildup that leads to obesity you have to choose a diet containing ingredients in their natural form or as close to their natural form as possible, as this is what the human body evolved for thousands of years to metabolize. This is the crux of the Paleolithic diet and this book will show you exactly what the Paleo diet is all about including:

- How it works
- How it came into being
- The foods you should eat while on the Paleo diet
- Foods you should avoid while on the Paleo diet
- The benefits you stand to derive when you follow the Paleo diet
- How to pair the Paleo diet with exercise
- Mistakes you should avoid while on the diet and much, much more!

By following this book, you will understand how the Paleolithic man was able to remain healthy, agile and fit so that you can model your life like his to stave off various health problems. Let's begin.

The Paleo Diet: A Comprehensive Background

Since this is a beginners' guide, we will start by building a strong understanding of what the diet is all about.

What is it?

The word Paleo diet comes from "Paleolithic Diet," a term used to refer to a dietary lifestyle that is rapidly becoming popular globally. The diet, considered to reflect what our ancestors ate, has been attributed to many benefits. Among them are boosting energy levels, weight loss and healing ailments linked to poor dietary lifestyles. The premise of the diet is simple; if the Paleolithic man didn't eat something, don't eat it either and if he ate something, you are free to eat it as well.

During the caveman's era, our ancestors were thought to only eat game or wild meat, nuts, poultry, seafood and fruits such as berries. Grains and dairy were unheard of during those days, as humans had not yet started practicing agriculture.

Interestingly, the caveman didn't suffer from health problems that we have today like cancer and diabetes. This shows there was something about the Paleolithic way of life that kept these health complications away.

What could that be? Well, while there might be many contributing factors, one of the things that stands out is the fact that food did not go through genetic modification to increase yield. There was no need for processing to enhance shelf life or add value and there was no need to domesticate animals or practice agriculture since food was in plenty. This means the food was very natural and free from insecticides, pesticides and other harmful chemicals since it existed in nature without the Paleolithic man's interference/input. This worked in his favor, as the body had evolved for hundreds of thousands of years until it was fully capable of utilizing the various components in such foods. As such, the toxic waste I mentioned earlier was nonexistent and as such, weight problems hardly existed.

Agriculture (planting various crops and domestication) didn't start until around 10,000 years ago. This is the time that humans started growing grains and started consuming dairy. Then fast forward to the 1700s and 1800s when the industrial revolution started. This marked the beginning of a series of events that saw more changes being done to food production to increase yield, increase resistance and quicken maturity. The use of pesticides, insecticides, fertilizers, fungicides and other substances increased. And after harvesting, processing of food started taking place. Some substances are now added to food to increase shelf life, to change color, to change taste and any other number of reasons. And since then, the trend has not stopped: we consume more factory-made or modified foods than ever before. And what has been the result? Well, the result has been a wide array of health complications that have plagued our society like never before because our bodies have not yet evolved to a point of fully metabolizing the foods that we eat these days. In fact, our body treats some of these foods as toxins, which explains why we face the health complications that we have these days. The Paleo diet seeks to eliminate the modern foods that are likely to cause various health problems and instead focuses on eating what our Paleolithic ancestors ate. Eliminating foods like refined sugar, dairy, grains, cereals, salt and replacing them with natural foods like grass fed meat, olive oil, nuts, seeds, vegetables and fruits.

Let's take it further by discussing the specific foods you are allowed to eat and those you are not allowed to eat while on the Paleo diet.

Foods to Eat

1. Paleo diet meats

By definition, almost all meats fall in the Paleo diet i.e. game meat, poultry, red meat and white meat. The rule of the thumb is to buy fresh meats rather than those that have been marinated, batter-coated or breaded. Also, choose meat from pastured animals to avoid toxins associated with non-organically raised animals e.g. given antibiotics.

Enjoy organic meats such as:

- Bison (bison jerky, bison sirloin, bison steaks, etc.)
- Buffalo
- Chicken (chicken breast, chicken thighs, chicken wings, eggs, etc.)
- Elk
- Emu
- Goat
- Goose
- Beef (steak, ground beef, New York steak, chuck steak, beef jerky, etc.)
- Kangaroo

- Lamb (lamb chops, lamb rack, etc.)
- Ostrich
- Pheasant
- Pork (bacon, pork chops, pork tenderloin, etc.)
- Poultry
- Quail
- Rabbit
- Rattlesnake
- Turkey
- Turtle
- Veal (lean veal)
- Venison
- Wild boar

2. Paleo diet fish and shellfish

Fish are one of the most important foods in the Paleo diet, and they are packed with great nutrients such as omega 3 fatty acids. The following fish and seafood are top picks for the Paleo diet:

- Bass
- Clams
- Crab
- Crawfish
- Crayfish
- Halibut
- Lobster
- Mackerel
- Mussels
- Oysters
- Red snapper
- Salmon
- Sardines
- Scallops

- Shark
- Shrimp
- Sunfish
- Swordfish
- Tilapia
- Trout
- Tuna

3. Paleo diet oils and fats

Contrary to the common belief that reducing fat intake facilitates weight loss, this has proven not to be the case for a number of reasons. First, fats tend to be very satiating compared to carbohydrates, which means that if you eat them, you won't have the urge to eat as often as if you had eaten carbohydrates. This essentially means you end up consuming less calories. That's not all; eating more fats and oils means that you will effectively eat less carbohydrates. As a result, you reduce your insulin production. Having high levels of insulin hormone in the body has been shown to put the body in a state of fat storage.. In fact, high insulin levels favor a process referred to as glycolysis i.e. fat creation. However, if you eat fewer carbohydrates, you end up producing lower levels of insulin, which in turn helps you to stop storing fats.

The following is a list of some of the best Paleo fats and oils for additional energy when trying to lose weight:

- Avocado oil

- Coconut oil

- Olive oil

4. Veggies

When it comes to veggies, the list is endless. All you need is to choose colored non-starchy veggies such as kales and tomatoes. The rule of the thumb is to eat leafy green veggies and whole fruits rather than starchy veggies, fruit juices and processed salads that contain added sugars. Eat any of these food groups as long as they are organically grown or unprocessed, and contain no added sweeteners or chemicals.

Here are a few you should enjoy:

- Asparagus
- Broccoli
- Brussels sprouts
- Cabbage
- Carrots
- Cauliflower
- Celery
- Collard greens
- Eggplant
- Green onion
- Kale

- Parsley
- Peppers
- Spinach
- Tomatoes

In addition to the above you are also free to eat the following root vegetables:

- Artichokes
- Beets
- Carrots
- Cassava
- Parsnips
- Radish
- Rutabaga
- Sweet potatoes
- Turnips
- Yams

Squashes are also a great addition to the diet:

- Acorn squash
- Buttercup squash
- Butternut squash
- Pumpkin
- Spaghetti squash
- Yellow crookneck squash
- Yellow summer squash
- Zucchini

Mushrooms are also in this category. Therefore, feel free to eat:

- Button mushroom
- Chantarelle mushroom
- Crimini mushroom
- Morel mushroom
- Oyster mushroom
- Porcini mushroom
- Portabello mushroom
- Shiitake mushroom

5. Paleo diet fruits

Fruits are delicious and double up as a source of a wide range of nutrients. However, fruits tend to be rich in fructose, which is still sugar. Therefore, it is advisable to cut back on your fruit intake if you are trying to lose weight on a Paleo diet. That said; feel free to indulge in a serving or two of fruit per day. Here is a list of Paleo-approved fruits:

- Apples
- Avocado
- Bananas
- Blackberries
- Blueberries
- Cantaloupe
- Figs
- Grapes
- Guava
- Lemon
- Lime
- Lychee

- Mango
- Oranges
- Papaya
- Peaches
- Pineapple
- Plums
- Raspberries
- Strawberries
- Tangerines
- Watermelon

6. Paleo diet nuts

These are a good choice for snacks as they contain high quantities of unsaturated fats that are heart-healthy. However, due to being high in calories, you should moderate the intake of nuts to a handful a day. Also, avoid those honey-roasted or candied and heavily salted nuts. You can choose varieties of seeds and nuts from these suggestions:

- Almonds
- Cashews

- Hazelnuts
- Macadamia nuts
- Pecans
- Pine nuts
- Pumpkin seeds
- Sunflower seeds
- Walnuts

Note: Since peanuts are not technically a type of nut, they do not make it onto the Paleo list.

7. Natural spices and herbs

Most Paleo foods do not require added preservatives, and can be stored through traditional methods such as freezing, canning, salting, smoking and fermentation. However if spices are your thing, go for those with no additives such as chili hot peppers, cinnamon and other natural sweeteners.

Here is the full list:

- Basil
- Bay leaves
- Black pepper
- Chilies
- Chives
- Cinnamon
- Cloves
- Coriander (fresh and seeds)
- Cumin
- Dill
- Fennel seeds
- Fresh parsley
- Garlic
- Horseradish
- Hot peppers
- Lavender
- Mint
- Nutmeg

- Nutmeg
- Onions
- Rosemary
- Salt
- Smoked paprika
- Star anise
- Tarragon
- Thyme
- Vanilla

Foods Not to Eat

The following list is a comprehensive collection of all the foods you should try to avoid while on the Paleo diet to lose weight. Chances are you will find it hard to keep yourself from eating these in the beginning, but once you get the hang of it, it becomes much easier.

Moreover, you are also likely to find much better substitutes for these foods.

Dairy

- Cheese
- Cottage cheese
- Cream cheese
- Dairy spreads
- Frozen yogurt
- Ice cream
- Milk (low-fat milk, 2% milk, whole milk, powdered milk, ice milk, etc.)
- Non-fat dairy creamer
- Pudding
- Yogurt

Fruit Juices and Soft Drinks

These are high in sugar and can upset your quest to losing weight, so stay away from them. In fact, soft drinks such as coke are full of high fructose corn syrup and sugar, and are therefore not Paleo friendly. Some of the juices and soft drinks to avoid include:

- Apple juice
- Coke
- Fanta
- Grape juice
- Mango juice
- Monster energy drink
- Mountain Dew
- Orange juice
- Pepsi
- Red bull
- Sprite
- Strawberry juice

Grains

Avoid anything that typically has grains in it. These include rice, wheat, barley and oats along with products that come from them such as crackers, bagels, cereal, pasta, granola bars and bread. Simply avoid every type of food that has grains in it, whether whole-grain, processed grains or whatever kind of grains you come across. Instead, try almond or coconut flour; these are low carb, high fiber, and protein rich.

Here is a list of some grains to avoid:

- Bread
- Cereals
- Corn
- Corn syrup (high-fructose corn syrup)
- Crackers
- Cream of wheat
- English muffins
- Hash browns
- Lasagna
- Oatmeal
- Pancakes

- Pasta
- Sandwiches
- Toast
- Wheat
- Wheat Thins

Legumes

Here are the ones you should stay away from:

Beans

- Adzuki beans
- Black beans
- Broad beans
- Fava beans
- Garbanzo beans
- Green beans
- Horse beans
- Kidney beans
- Lima beans
- Navy beans
- Pinto beans

- Red beans
- String beans
- White beans

Peas

- Black-eyed peas
- Chickpeas
- Snow peas
- Sugar snap peas

Peanuts

- All soybean products and derivatives
- Lentils
- Mesquite
- Miso
- Peanut butter
- Soybeans
- Tofu

Artificial sweeteners

By definition, no artificial sweeteners are included in the Paleo diet. If you want to sweeten your foods, use maple syrup, honey, or Stevia instead.

Fatty meats, snacks, and salty foods

Avoid processed foods, those with too much salt, or other quick snacks that come in a packaged form. For example, if you want to eat meat, just go for some steak, but stay away from these fatty foods:

- Chips
- Cookies
- French fries
- Hot dogs
- Ketchup
- Pastries
- Pretzels
- Wheat Thins

Alcohol

Alcohol is a gluten product and for this reason is not included in the Paleo diet. This includes, but is not limited to:

- Alcohol and mixers
- Beer
- Rum
- Tequila
- Vodka
- Whiskey

The list of foods to eat and those to avoid is undoubtedly long. What you might be wondering is; are there some foods that you should make the center of your diet to derive the most benefits? We will discuss up to 20 foods that you should strive to include in your diet to help you get started.

If you like to find out more about Paleo Diet and learn how to cook tons of tasty and more important healthy recipes, got your 4-Week Meal Plan and 4-Week Work Out Plan you can simply follow the link below and buy it on Amazon:

Go **ladypannana.com/ebooks/paleo1**

to get **an E-Book** version on Amazon

Go **ladypannana.com/books/paleo1**

to get **a Paperback** version on Amazon

Go **ladypannana.com/audiobooks**

to get **an Audio** version on Audible (There are NO recipes)

Mediterranean Diet: Mediterranean Cookbook For Beginners, Lose Weight And Get Healthy

Have you ever thought about changing your unhealthy eating habits but you simply couldn't because you didn't know how? Or have you ever felt like your body has been imprisoned with excessive weight that won't just go away? If your answer to any of the two questions is yes, then today is your lucky day. This is because this book will introduce you to what will be the solution to your weight loss and health issues.

So what is this big solution? Mediterranean diet is what I am talking about. In 2017, the U.S News and World Report rated this diet as the second best die. The reason why it was highly rated is because it has numerous health benefits. Some of them include its ability to prevent diseases like dementia, cancer, diabetes and others, its powerful influence on promoting weight loss and its effectiveness in boosting your overall health. What is also cool about this diet is that you still get to eat delicious food and does not impose strict rules, which makes it quite flexible.

If you are ready to change your life for the better and adopt a healthy lifestyle, then adopting the Mediterranean diet is the best decision you could ever make. Thanks to this book, you will have all the information you need to get started with the book.

Here is a preview of what you will learn:

- What the Mediterranean diet is
- Where it originated from
- How it works
- How it is beneficial to your health
- What to eat in order to reap the health benefits
- What steps you will need to take to adopt it
- Many tasty recipes that you can try

Understanding The Mediterranean Diet

As a beginner you are probably wondering what a Mediterranean diet is. Don't worry, that question is going to be extensively answered in this chapter. But that's not the only thing this chapter will do. It will also try to give you a better understanding of what the Mediterranean is looking at its origins and how it works.

So what is the Mediterranean diet?

The Mediterranean diet is based on the traditional foods that people who lived in the Mediterranean countries like Greece, Spain and Italy used to eat back in 1940s and 1950s. Although the word Mediterranean is accompanied by the word diet, it is not really a diet but rather an eating lifestyle that requires you to eat meals which are high on plant based foods (like legumes, vegetables, seeds, nuts, whole grains and fruits), moderate to high on fish and moderate on dairy products like yogurt and cheese. While on the diet, you can also occasionally drink red wine and red meat or non fish meat products.

That said, the Mediterranean diet is not only about food, it is also about lifestyle. When you are on a Mediterranean diet you are supposed to imitate the lifestyle of the people from the Mediterranean region. This means you should be physically active and practice the art of enjoying the social experience of eating as the diet requires you to adopt a habit of slowing down when eating to take pleasure in each bite you take. It also requires you to share meals with family and friends as much as you possibly can.

Now, it is very important for you to take some time to know where the diet came from before you can jump right into it. So what is its story?

Brief History of the Mediterranean Diet

As the name suggests, the Mediterranean diet originated from the culinary traditions found in the Mediterranean region, more specifically from Italy and Greece.

Hundreds of years ago, the Mediterranean region was the site of ancient and advanced civilization. It hosted different people who included the Persians, Babylonians, Assyrians and Sumerians who settled on the valley of the Nile that stretched on its banks.

Over the years, more people started migrating to the Mediterranean region and soon the Cretans came in and rose to power. They were followed by Phoenicians, learned Greeks and finally the emerging power of Rome. The territory was then divided into East and West. The process of exchanging powers that happened in the past where Phoenicians overturned the Cretans and the Greeks overturned the Phoenicians resulted into a region that had different cultures, religions and beliefs. Slowly by slowly the people in the region integrated and started modifying each other's customs, language and religions.

They also modified their eating habits through their partial integration. Back then, the Greeks practiced agriculture where they farmed and produced vegetables (like mushrooms, chicory, lettuce, mallow and leeks), olives, which they used to make olive oil, and grapes, which they used to make wine. They also identified with bread.

On the other side, the Romans fished and ate plenty of fish. They were huge lovers of fish and sea foods like oysters. They all didn't eat a lot of beef or dairy products because the climate of the region did not favor the upbringing of grazing animals. As the years went by, the Romans, Greeks and other cultures started adopting each other's foods to a point that the Mediterranean region had an almost similar diet.

The discovery of the Mediterranean diet

In 1960s, a nutritionist by the name of Ancel Keys noted that people who lived in the Mediterranean region especially in the mountain of Crete experienced low rates of cancer and heart diseases. He also discovered that these people lived long. Ancel was curious and so he decided to carry out a research that compares the health of the people from the Mediterranean region to the health of the people from other regions like the U.S, Japan and others.

Ancel did what is now known as a seven-nation study. In this study, he examined how different diets from different regions affected the mortality and disease rates of the people in those areas. In his studies, he looked at United States, Netherlands, Italy, Japan, Finland and Greece. After the study was through, Ancel Keys discovered that people who ate foods from the Mediterranean region, which is now known as the Mediterranean diet had the lowest disease and death rates.

In 1975, Ancel Keys and his collaborator who was also his wife Margaret Keys publicized the Mediterranean diet in the U.S. Their effort to make the diet known was not that successful. Not until 1990s when Walter Willet who was from Harvard University school of public health presented the diet to the world.

Over the past few decades, the diet has gained a lot of popularity and it is now considered as one of the healthiest diets on earth. But why is it one of the best diets in the world? The answer lays in the science behind how it works.

How the Mediterranean Diet Works

In the world today, we have numerous diets, which all preach the gospel of weight loss and better health. The truth of the matter is that most of these diets do not actually work and if they do they are not sustainable because they go against how we were built as natural eating beings by imposing starvation on us. That is why a lot of us shut down when the word diet is mentioned.

So is the Mediterranean just another scam that has come? The answer is NO. The Mediterranean diet is quite different from other diets that you may have followed in the past for the purpose of losing weight or improving your health. This is because the Mediterranean diet was first of all never designed for disease prevention or weight loss. It was just an old lifestyle of eating that evolved naturally over the years inspired by the foods that were available in Mediterranean region; and during that period people from outside the region started noticing how healthy the people from the Mediterranean region were. They also discovered how easy it was to lose weight when they tried the diet.

In short the Mediterranean diet unlike other diets was discovered after it was seen to have positive effects on people's health and weight and the amazing part is that people followed the diet each and every day comfortably from when they were born to the day that they died. This was mainly because the diet is not restrictive to a point that one cannot keep up with it, as there are no food groups that are completely off limits and you really don't have to track your food intake. That's how great the diet is.

So why does this diet work so well? What is the science behind it?

The science behind the Mediterranean diet is a pretty easy concept. The diet just uses an overall diet approach where it presents you with a combination of powerful foods that are both super nutritious and healthy. Let me break it down for you.

Normally there are those foods that are considered super foods because they have greater significance on your health. A good example of these foods include salmon which contains omega 3 fatty acids that helps you reduce the risk of cardiovascular diseases, Spinach which contains anti-inflammatory and antioxidants properties that help in promoting your vision and your bone health and liver which helps your body lower its cholesterol levels and reduce the risk of diseases like cancers.

Most of the times when we are on our unhealthy conventional diets, we cheat ourselves that we are eating healthy just because we have added one of the aforementioned super foods like salmon in our diet. The truth of the matter is that one addition of the super foods does not make the whole meal healthy. In fact you will hardly get a noticeable healthy benefit when you do so.

The reason why the Mediterranean diet is so healthy and powerful is because it adjusts your whole diet and makes it a huge combination of super foods which are so important for good health. Actually, the secret behind the Mediterranean diet is in what its food adds to your health. As you now know, the diet usually bases its meals on vegetables, fruits, whole grains and healthy fats.

The heart healthy fats like olive oil normally have lower levels of LDL (low density lipoprotein). The lower level of LDL helps reduce the plaque built up in your arteries and cholesterol in your body. When it comes to whole grains, they are high in fiber, which controls your digestion and blood sugar.

The Mediterranean diet also requires you to incorporate fish into your meals at least twice a week and that provides your body with omega 3 fatty acids, which provides your body with the good cholesterol HDL. The fruits and vegetables provide you with valuable antioxidants, which protect your body against diseases such as cancer. That is generally how the Mediterranean diet works.

As you have seen, the Mediterranean diet is healthy and it works. But just to clear any doubt of shadow of whether the diet works or not we are going to look at some of the researches that have been done on Mediterranean diet and see how effective the diet was when it was put to test. Two studies show the Mediterranean diet works perfectly. Here they are:

In 2013, a study was carried out in Spain, which tried to figure out the connection between the Mediterranean diet and cardiovascular health. The study was done by the University of Barcelona. This study involved over 7,000 Spanish participants who were either smokers, diabetic or overweight. The participants were told to adopt the Mediterranean style of eating which consisted of healthy fats like nuts and olive oils for 5 years. Just before the participants reached the 5 years mark, a comprehensive follow up on their health was done and they were seen to have a huge improvement in their health. The improvement was so huge that the study was closed there and then.

This is what the researchers found. The participants who were at high risk of contracting cardiovascular diseases had a risk reduction of up to 30%. This study was later published in the New England journal of medicine where people were shocked at just how beneficial the diet was to their health.

Another study about the Mediterranean diet was published in the British Journal of Nutrition in 2012. The study suggested that the diet had the ability to lower heart disease risk. It attributed this to the decrease of the so called bad cholesterol LDL that comes with following the Mediterranean diet. The study also suggested that there is a link between the Mediterranean diet and a low risk of cancer.

Those two studies prove that the Mediterranean diet works.

If you like to find out more about Mediterranean Diet and learn how to cook tons of tasty and more important healthy recipes, got your Meal Plan you can simply follow the link below and buy it on Amazon:

Go   ladypannana.com/ebook/mediterranean1

to get **an E-Book** version on Amazon

Go

ladypannana.com/books/mediterranean1

to get **a Paperback** version on Amazon

Go **ladypannana.com/audiobook**

to get **an Audio** version on Audible (There are NO recipes)

ABOUT THE AUTHOR

The goal of "Lady Pannana" Publishing Company is to provide you with easy-to-cook, authentic, and tasty recipes.

To increase your health, energy, and well-being, Lady Pannana cookbooks bring together the best of international cuisines and teach you how to cook them in the comfort of your own home.

From special diets to international treats, pick up a cookbook today and lose yourself in a whole new world of possibilities.

No mealtime should be boring, so go ahead and treat yourself!

Browse our catalog of titles and don't forget to tell us what you think about our books. We want to create a better experience for our readers. Your voice, your opinion, and your input only serve to ensure that the next time you pick up a Lady Pannana Publishing Title, it will be better than the last!

To find out more about Healthy Cooking and Recipes visit our blog below

Visit Our Blog => ladypannana.com

You can also stay up-to-date with what's going on here by subscribing for free updates, liking Lady Pannana on FaceBook, or following us on Instagram, Twitter etc.

FaceBook: ladypannana.com/facebook

Twitter: ladypannana.com/twitter

Instagram: ladypannana.com/instagram

Pinterest: ladypannana.com/pinterest

Tumbler: ladypannana.com/tumblr

Google+: ladypannana.com/google

YouTube: ladypannana.com/youtube

LinkedIn: ladypannana.com/linkedin

Visit **our author page** on Amazon to see other work done by Lady Pannana.

ladypannana.com/amazonauthor

If you have any questions or suggestions feel free to contact us at

ladypannana@gmail.com

Thank you for taking the time to read this and we look forward to seeing you on the blog sometime soon!

Cheers,

Lady Pannana

Wait! Before You Continue... Would You Like to Get Healthier, Happier and Enjoy Eating at the Same Time?

Would You Like to Increase Your Overall Well-Being?

If you answered YES, you are not alone. We believe almost everyone wants to have a good body and be healthy by simply start eating clean and diet. Unfortunately, most of us have no idea how to do it. Yes, dieting can work, but starving yourself just leads to frustration and failure. Also, dieting will not help your health! It will just harm you. What we recommend you here it isn't dieting, it is a LIFESTYLE!

Right now, you can get full **FREE access to Low-Carb eBook+Paleo Report to Learn How to Cook Tasty and More Important HEALTHY Recipes,**

so you can easily and quickly start pursuing your goals.

Low - carb eating is something that has become increasingly popular in recent years. It has been linked with a range of health benefits including:

- Improved weight loss (even when you're not consciously restricting your calories).
- Improved concentration.
- Increased energy levels.
- Prevention and treatment of various chronic diseases.
- Reduced blood glucose levels (which are particularly beneficial for diabetics).
- Reduced blood pressure.

Free Bonus

Go Here to Get Instant Access

ladypannana.com/freebook

Made in the USA
Monee, IL
14 October 2024

67830281R00154